Irrigation and Society
in the Peruvian Desert

Irrigation and Society in the Peruvian Desert

The Puquios of Nasca

Katharina Schreiber and Josué Lancho Rojas

LEXINGTON BOOKS
Lanham • Boulder • New York • Oxford

LEXINGTON BOOKS

Published in the United States of America
by Lexington Books
An imprint of The Rowman & Littlefield Publishing Group, Inc.
4501 Forbes Boulevard, Suite 200, Lanham, Maryland 20706

PO Box 317
Oxford
OX2 9RU, UK

British Library Cataloguing in Publication Information Available

Library of Congress Cataloging-in-Publication Data

Schreiber, Katharina Jeanne.
    Irrigation and society in the Peruvian desert : the puquios of Nasca / Katharina
Schreiber and Josue Lancho Rojas.
        p. cm.
    Includes bibliographical references and index.
    ISBN 0-7391-0641-4 (cloth : alk. paper)
    1. Nazca culture. 2. Indians of South America—Irrigation—Peru—Ica (Dept.)
    3. Irrigation—Peru—Ica (Dept.) 4. Ica (Peru : Dept.)—Antiquities. I. Lancho Rojas,
Josue. II. Title.

    F3429.1.N3S37 2003
    985'.27019—dc21   2003005638

Printed in the United States of America

Dedicated to the memory of Juan Luis Montoya Valenzuela.

CONTENTS

LIST OF FIGURES

LIST OF TABLES

FOREWORD

Vernon L. Scarborough

Ancient Peruvian social complexity is known by several unique characteristics, perhaps the most perplexing of which remains the absence of a formal writing system. One of the least mentioned technical attributes, permitting the extreme degree to which they were able to engineer their environment, was their ability to access a buried water table from an otherwise parched desert setting. The sunken gardens, or "mahamaes," first announced to a broad Americanist audience with the publication of Parsons's reports in *American Antiquity* (1968; Parsons and Psuty 1975), demonstrate the energy expended and labor directed in the excavations several meters below the surface to establish farming plots immediately above the water table. The great Chimu capital of ancient Chan Chan maintained several sunken gardens (Moseley 1983), though the antiquity of the technique is likely even greater.

Recently, Fairley (2003) reports on the use of "geological water storage" identified with runoff directed into embanked soils underlain by impervious bedrock, soils with a porosity and thickness to hold significant amounts of water behind a human-made wall or dam. He argues that the wall buttress containing the moistened sediments had a diminutive hole or deliberate break from which water filtered. Fairley indicates an Inka association for his specific site, though this design feature is likely to have an earlier manifestation.

Puquios represent another kind of water table use. "A puquio is . . . a horizontal well: an open trench and/or a subterranean gallery that connects a point on the surface with subsurface water. The underground water filters into the puquio, flows through it, and empties into either a small reservoir *(kocha)* or directly into irrigation canals. Puquios provide not only a reliable source of irrigation water, but also a year-round supply of domestic water" (this volume, 36).

Many of us interested in ancient water management globally have only recently become aware of the puquio systems within the Andean rain shadow of southern Peru and northern Chile. The first mention of the puquio system was apparently made in the underreported field notes of Alfred Kroeber in 1926 (this volume, 51), though puquios were known and discussed by several Spanish sources by the 1930s. Nevertheless, not until now is a systematic analysis of these systems performed. In this monograph, Katharina Schreiber and Josué Lancho Rojas carefully examine the puquio remains from the Nasca region of southwestern Peru. They skillfully incorporate aspects of ethnohistory, ethnoarchaeology, and controlled archaeological

xv

foot survey in establishing the distribution and significance of these systems. By examining a sizable portion of an entire ancient culture area—the Nasca—Schreiber places the puquio system in a holistic and anthropological context, and she provides an empirical rationale for the system's antiquity.

Although several archaic states arose in desert settings, few occupied as arid a setting as southern coastal and piedmont Peru. Rainfall in the Nasca region is not measurable in most years. In order to make a living, to say nothing about securing a simple drink of potable water, the Nasca culture invested heavily in puquio construction. The argument for ancient Peruvians inventing this technology is one of the most compelling aspects of this monograph. Schreiber's examination of over forty puquio systems from three discrete but adjacent environments demonstrates that puquios were initiated by AD 400-500. She shows that a naturally occurring Zone of Infiltration, recharged primarily from surface flowing streams with sources in the Andes, abuts an inhospitable, lower-lying Middle Valley Zone identified by an absence of surface water. At the Zone of Infiltration, most surface sources are absorbed into the sands and related alluvial soils until they migrate underground to issue at the surface again for a relatively short distance within a yet Lower Valley environment. In a convincing argument based on hard-won field data, the authors demonstrate that aboriginal occupation of the extremely arid Middle Valley Zone flourished by AD 500, an environment impossible to dwell without sophisticated water control. Puquio construction is the only way this relatively flat, open, and subsequently productive setting was agriculturally transformed to support the populations of antiquity.

Schreiber and Lancho's data set points out the frequent association of present-day puquios with small reservoirs or *kochas*. Ancient Peruvian water systems elsewhere seldom mention the role of tank construction in connection with elaborate canalization efforts, especially to the immediate north. Given evaporation rates, *kochas* may be a later addition to the puquio systems, though survey elsewhere in Peru might further assess the role of still water surface exposures in the ancient past given Schreiber and Lancho's present-day observations.

Conventional wisdom outside Peru suggests that the puquio system was a colonial period introduction from Spain, given the elaborate and unique characteristics of horizontal wells and their much longer history among desert civilizations of the Old World (Barnes and Fleming 1991; cf. Scarborough 2003). The *karez* or *qanat* of the Old World continues to operate along a narrow belt from south-central China to Mediterranean North Africa and Spain. The Old World karez was likely spread widely by the ancient Persians, with the oldest known reference to the technique identified on a cuneiform clay tablet associated with Sargon II of Assyria (722-705 BC) (Garbrecht 1987: 8). Tunnel conduits for directing the flow of water were also associated with sixth-century BC Jerusalem (Gill 1991) as well as Persepolis (English 1966), and the Greeks are credited with a lengthy water passageway through a karstic hill at Samos at about the same time (Crouch 1993: fig. 4.1). *Karez* construction was extended to Spain by the Moors and likely influenced a set of modifications made to New World horizontal wells. Schreiber argues that the indigenous puquio systems of the Nasca were constructed as open trenches, subsequently filled in over a framework of wooden lintels and support stones preserving the underground conduit. Likely no deeper than ten meters, these features were made accessible by periodically positioning rock-lined, vertical *ojos,* or shafts, down to the moving water conduit. Although this type of construction may occur in the Old World, by far the most pervasive construction technique was/is the tunneling through homogeneous alluvial and colluvial clays. And many of these latter systems are deep; the deepest at Gonabad in Iran, near the Afghan border, with a "mother well" descending to 300 meters below the arid surface, though most are excavated in the range of 20-100 meters (English 1966). This construction technique differs markedly from the trenching adaptation that Schreiber describes in the Nasca region, though tunnel excavation is frequently appended to these latter systems today. As the authors indicate, Spanish technology surely influenced the ancient puquios and may well have introduced the classic "galleria" system of excavated tunnels.

Recent work by Monica Barnes (2002) in the Tehuacan Valley, Mexico, may suggest that those systems are colonial in date. In Mexico, they do appear to be tunneled gallerias, not filled-in trench systems (Woodbury and Neely 1972). Nevertheless, until the kind of settlement pattern and land-use investigations are initiated, like those conducted by Schreiber in Nasca, a true test of the antiquity of the Tehuacan Valley systems remains undone.

Mesoamerica has a long ideological tradition of water use associated with mountain interiors, water issuing from specific "water mountains." This deeply entrenched worldview was present among the Aztec (Broda, Carrasco, and Matos M. 1982), the Maya (Scarborough 1998), and likely the ancient Peruvians. Schreiber notes the mythology associated with Cerro Blanco, the sandy mountain containing a subterranean lake and the projected source for most of the puquios of the Nasca region. This origin myth is an enduring and deeply embedded cultural construct throughout much of the Americas.

Katharina Schreiber's and Josué Lancho Rojas's monograph is the definitive statement about this type of water management, not only for Peru but also for the New World. When coupled with the other uniquely Peruvian techniques for obtaining subsurface water in antiquity, it reveals the degree of water table manipulation by this great set of South American civilizations. I know of no other ancient culture as knowledgeable about their water table or as technologically clever at harvesting it. Schreiber and Lancho's work adds considerably to our corpus of technological know-how incorporated by ancient society and further accents the innovative and independent developments of the indigenous populations of the New World.

References Cited

Barnes, Monica. 2002. "Tehuacan Filtration Galleries in Pan-Hispanic Perspective." Paper presented in a symposium on the prehispanic fossilized canal systems of the Tehuacan Valley, organized by James B. Neely. Society for American Archaeology, Denver.

Barnes, Monica, and David Fleming. 1991. "Filtration-Gallery Irrigation in the Spanish New World." *Latin American Antiquity* 2: 48-68.

Broda, J., D. Carrasco, and E. Matos M. 1982. *The Great Temple of Tenochtitlan, Center and Periphery in the Aztec World.* Berkeley: University of California Press.

Crouch, Dora P. 1993. *Water Management in Ancient Greek Cities.* Oxford: Oxford University Press.

English, Paul W. 1966. *City and Village in Iran: Settlement and Economy in the Kirman Basin.* Madison: University of Wisconsin Press.

Fairley, Jr., Jerry P. 2003. "Geological Water Storage in Pre-Columbian Peru." *Latin American Antiquity* 14.

Garbrecht, G. 1987. "Irrigation throughout History: Problems and Solutions." In *Water for the Future*, edited by W. O. Wunderlich and J. E. Prins, 3-18. Boston: A.A. Balkema.

Gill, Daniel. 1991. "Subterranean Waterworks of Biblical Jerusalem: An Adaptation of a Karst System." *Science* 254: 1467-70.

Moseley, Michael E. 1983. "The Good Old Days Were Better: Agrarian Collapse and Tectonics." *American Anthropologist* 85: 773-799.

Parsons, Jeffrey R. 1968. "The Archaeological Significance of Mahamaes Cultivation on the Coast of Peru." *American Antiquity* 33: 80-85.

Parsons, Jeffrey R., and Norbert P. Psuty. 1975. "Sunken Fields and Prehispanic Subsistence on the Peruvian Coast." *American Antiquity* 40: 259-282.

Scarborough, Vernon L. 1998. "Ecology and Ritual: Water Management and the Maya." *Latin American Antiquity* 9: 135-159.

_____. 2003. *The Flow of Power: Ancient Water Systems and Landscapes.* Santa Fe: School of American Research Press.

Woodbury, Robert B., and James A. Neely. 1972. "Water Control Systems of the Tehuacan Valley." In *Chronology and Irrigation: The Prehistory of the Tehuacan Valley.* Vol. 4, edited by F. Johnson, 81-153. Austin: University of Texas Press.

ACKNOWLEDGMENTS

We would like to thank the institutions and individuals who provided the financial support that enabled us to carry out our initial studies of the puquios in 1986: CONCYTEC and CORDEICA (Lancho) and University Research Expeditions (Schreiber). Subsequent archaeological research and follow-up studies of the puquios were funded by the National Geographic Society (1989-90, and 1995-96), the Kaplan Fund (1994), and the Academic Senate of the University of California at Santa Barbara (1987, 1988, 1993). María and Renate Reiche also contributed funds to the support of the project.

We thank Professor John Rowe for encouraging us to undertake our study of the puquios, and for his continued support. We thank our archaeological colleagues for their years of support of our studies: Luis Lumbreras, Giuseppe Orefici, Federico Kauffman, Fernando Silva Santisteban, Miguel Pazos, Susana Arce, Anita Cook, Helaine Silverman, and Patrick Carmichael. Johny Isla served as codirector of the archaeological projects of 1994 and 1996, and he could not have been a better colleague or friend. Student participants on the projects included Mary Van Buren and Cynthia Bettison (1986); Dennis Ogburn, David McDowell, and Jeffrey Cox (1990); Huayta Montoya, Christina Conlee, Tiffiny Tung, April VanWyke, and Kirk Frye (1994); Giancarlo Marconi (1994, 1995); and Karen Anderson, Kevin Vaughn, Corina Kellner, Cynthia Herhahn, and Justin Jennings (1996). We thank also Keith Kintigh and twenty-one UREP volunteers for their participation in the 1986 puquio project.

In Nasca we thank our friends Aroldo Corzo, Professor Nestor Quincho, Graciela Caso and her sister Lucy, Angela Rojas, the brothers Orlando and Rogelio Aragonez and their beautiful families, Juan Valdivia, Eduardo Herrán, and Efraín Alegría. Teófilo Guía and Timoteo Gutiérrez of the Hotel Nazca Lines have made us feel welcome year after year. We owe a debt of gratitude to the small and valiant group of "limpiadores" of the millenarian puquios, headed by Pánfilo Farfán. And we thank our friend Olivia Watkin of Wasi Punku for creating a home for several teams of archaeologists.

We express our appreciation to colleagues who read and commented on earlier drafts of this work: Anita Cook, Chip Stanish, Patrick Carmichael, Helaine Silverman, Christina Conlee, Kevin Vaughn, and Hendrik Van Gijseghem. We owe a great debt to David Lawson of the Anthropology Graphics Laboratory at UCSB. David took our words, drawings, and photographs, and wove them into the fine copy seen here. He not only redrafted most of our original drawings, but also drew many others himself.

Finally, we thank our families for their understanding and unstinting support of our research and our love for the history of Peru.

CHAPTER 1

NASCA:
JEWEL OF THE PERUVIAN
SOUTH COAST

Nasca is a delight. Green and serene, it is the emerald of the south coast of Peru. An oasis in the desert today, a mecca to travelers from all over the world, Nasca was also home to one of the most distinctive prehispanic civilizations of the Andes, one that produced perhaps the finest and most elaborate ceramic and textile art ever known. Yet Nasca exists tucked amidst the arid western foothills of the Andes Mountains (figure 1.1), and sprawls across the rainless desert—one of the driest places on the face of the earth. How is this possible? How were the ancient people of Nasca able to conquer this harsh environment and transform it into the sparkling jewel that it remains today?

The rivers that flow westward out of the Andes and cross the deserts to the Pacific Ocean have been used for millennia by ancient and modern peoples all along coastal Peru to water their fields and slake their thirsts. But in Nasca only a trickle of water is bestowed upon the valleys by the mountain rains, and even that ceases to run most months of the year. And in many years the rivers do not flow at all. Rather than relying on the water in the rivers, then, the key to the accomplishments of past inhabitants of Nasca lay in their ability to tap into the water lying below the surface of the dry land, allowing the transformation of that surface into a green paradise.

The people of Nasca did this by developing an ingenious system of below-ground aqueducts, which today they call *puquios*.[1] Puquios[2] act essentially as horizontal wells: they tap subsurface water—from the phreatic layer, primarily the underground flow of the rivers—and transport that water to their homes and fields on the surface.

Perhaps this development is most charmingly described by the Englishman Clements Markham, who, as a young man in 1853, traveled south from Lima along the coast of Peru. When he reach Nasca he marveled at the verdant landscape and described it as "the most fertile and beautiful spot on the coast of Peru" (Markham

1

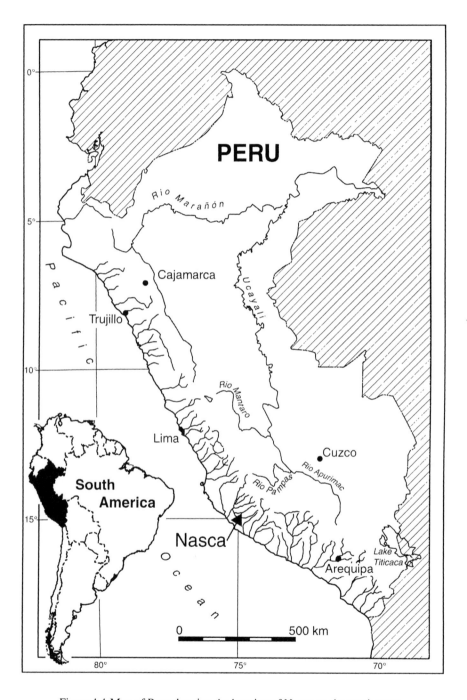

Figure 1.1 Map of Peru showing the location of Nasca on the south coast.

1991: 50). He found it particularly exceptional because the Nasca Valley seemed to be one of the driest places he had seen. How was this possible?

> The fertility [of Nasca] is due to the skill and industry of the ancient inhabitants. Under their care an arid wilderness was converted into a smiling paradise, and so it has continued. This was effected by cutting deep trenches along the whole length of the valley and so far up the mountains that the present inhabitants do not know the positions of their origin. High up the valley the main trenches (puquios) appear, some four feet in height, roofed over and floored with stones and also with stone sides. Descending from the mountains, these covered channels . . . supply . . . every hacienda with water all the year round and feed . . . the little streams which irrigate the fields and gardens. (Markham 1991: 50)

In this book we will describe for the reader the puquio system as it exists today, and as we believe it existed in the past. Elaborate hydraulic technology is no stranger to the ancient Andes, so we begin by summarizing some of the hydraulic accomplishments of various Andean cultures, from the simple canals of the earliest agriculturalists, to the great hydraulic works of the Chimú and the Incas. We follow this with a summary of the cultural history of Nasca: the rise and fall of the various cultures and civilizations, and their accomplishments. Only by understanding the history of the region, and the needs and abilities of those past societies, can we piece together the cultural context in which the puquios played a role.

In chapter 2, we shall discuss the physiographic context of the puquios. The physical setting of Nasca differentiates it from other coastal valleys, and provides a set of extreme constraints best ameliorated through the development of puquio technology. We shall spend some effort detailing the physical conditions—the geological and hydrological limitations imposed upon the people of Nasca by their physical world.

In chapter 3 we discuss the puquios themselves, in terms of their technology, their probable means of construction, and how they are used today. We summarize previous studies that have been made of the puquios, primarily in the 1920s, 1930s, and 1940s, and detail our own efforts made over the past two decades.

In chapters 4 through 8 we describe the system, detailing each puquio in the Nasca, Aja, Tierras Blancas, Taruga, and Las Trancas Irrigation Sectors. While there are some thirty-six puquios functioning at present, we believe their original number was somewhat higher—at least forty-one, and perhaps as many as fifty or more. To the extent possible, we also present evidence for puquios that no longer exist.

Perhaps the most crucial issue to archaeologists and historians is the question of the date of construction of the puquios. We will argue in chapter 9 that the archaeological data support a prehispanic date of construction of most or all of the puquios, during the first millennium AD, beginning during the period of transition between Early and Late Nasca culture. We also consider the possibility that some puquios were extensively modified after the Spanish conquest, during the colonial period or later.

Concluding that puquio technology was indeed used in prehispanic times, we reconsider the cultural history of Nasca, and place the puquios within their likely cultural contexts. We shall see that the time of initial puquio construction was a time of great cultural disruption and change in Nasca, and that cultural transformation and survival was made possible, at least in part, by the development of puquio technology. Finally, we reconsider the puquios in the modern world, their importance to Nasca, and their significance to our understanding and appreciation of traditional indigenous technology.

Hydraulic Technology in the Prehispanic Andes

Human populations require food, and food production—especially agriculture—requires a detailed knowledge of the natural environment and the constraints it places on the ability to produce food: temperature regimes, water availability, soil conditions, and so forth. It is often, if not usually, the case that human populations must manipulate their natural environment in order to provide conditions conducive to the production of food. In the case of the Andean sierra, human populations had to overcome limited and seasonal rainfall as well as low temperatures at higher altitudes in order to grow food. On the hyperarid coast, where rainfall is negligible, the lack of water placed serious constraints on the development of agricultural systems. As we shall see, prehispanic Andean cultures manipulated water and other factors, both in the sierra and on the coast, in a variety of ways and on a variety of scales, allowing them to produce food for ever-growing populations.

In considering human modifications of the natural environment, we need to address three interrelated issues. In the first place, these modifications are primarily adaptations to normal conditions, and normal, predictable fluctuations in those conditions. Second, these technological innovations may or may not be able to deal with extraordinary changes in normal conditions; extended droughts, for example, may result in agricultural collapse if the technology is not able to handle extreme conditions. And third, construction of such features requires human labor and organization, of varying degrees of complexity. This latter point is especially relevant to concerns about the development of complex social organization. It was argued, for example, by Wittfogel (1957) that the development of large-scale irrigation systems contributed directly to the emergence of complex social systems, which were needed to coordinate their construction and maintenance. Others (e.g., Adams 1974) have argued that complex social organizations preceded the development of large-scale irrigation systems. While our intent here is not to test such ideas, our data do provide another useful example of the role of large-scale irrigation in the emergence of sociopolitical complexity. We shall return to this issue in chapter 10.

The sophistication of prehispanic hydraulic technology in the Andes demonstrates that the Andean peoples had a very clear understanding of their environment, and how to manipulate it to their advantage. From the earliest agricultural communities of the coast to the impressive civilizations and empires of later millennia, the Andean people have been concerned with water—how to find it, how to distribute it, and how to control it. On the hyperarid coast of Peru this was accomplished both through the building of extensive systems of canal irrigation, and through tapping groundwater sources. In the highlands, where low temperatures were an additional factor detrimental to agriculture, the native populations developed ways of using water and terracing to raise ambient temperatures and to bring new areas under cultivation.

The first extensive agriculture on the coast of Peru probably pertains to the Late Archaic Period, also called the Cotton Preceramic, roughly 2500-1800 BC, a time when cotton and other industrial crops were grown along the Peruvian coast. Without the benefit of irrigation in at least some form, cultivation would have been extremely limited if indeed it was possible at all. In the following Initial Period (1800-800 BC), food production became the dominant form of subsistence, a development that could not have occurred without the concomitant development of canal irrigation. The first systems were probably relatively simple: short canals were diverted out of rivers, and the water directed across the adjacent fields. While we have no clear examples of irrigation systems dating to the Late Archaic and Initial Periods we can assume their existence based on the simple fact that agriculture could not have existed at that time without irrigation.

As time went by, populations grew, more land needed to be brought under cultivation, and irrigation systems grew accordingly, becoming larger and more complex, and leaving extensive remains still visible today. While we could cite innumerable examples of canal irrigation in all ensuing periods along the coast, this form of irrigation certainly reached its apogee with the Chimú culture of the north coast, dating to the Late Intermediate Period (AD 1000-1476). As Ortloff and others have amply demonstrated, the Chimú had an extremely sophisticated knowledge of engineering, and brought huge tracts of desert under cultivation through the construction of enormous irrigation canals (Kosok 1965; Ortloff 1981, 1988, 1993, 1995). In the event of severe climatic disruption, they even attempted to connect the Chicama Valley with the Moche Valley via a long-distance canal (Ortloff, Moseley, and Feldman 1982; Ortloff and Kolata 1993: 214-215), although the reasons for the lack of success of this venture are yet a matter of some dispute (Kus 1984; T. Pozorski and S. Pozorski 1982).

On a somewhat smaller scale, where groundwater (the phreatic zone) was close to the surface, agricultural fields were excavated down into the ground to a level slightly above the phreatic layer (Denevan 1980; Parsons and Psuty 1974, 1975; Rowe 1969; Soldi 1982). Such fields, called *hoyas* or *mahamaes* (or even *puquios*), were watered by the rising of the subsurface water through capillary action. *Hoyas* were found most commonly near the coast, where the water table is relatively high. Good examples can still be seen today on the north coast, especially those adjacent to the Chimú capital at Chan Chan. Other large expanses have been identified south of Lima in the Chilca Valley, as well as in the Pisco Valley. Restricted in geographic extent, *hoyas* probably played a secondary role to canal irrigation (Moseley 1969), and, indeed, this technology may not have developed until after AD 500 (Parsons and Psuty 1974, 1975).

It is interesting that a similar technology was in use in Arab North Africa, in the Algerian Sahara near the Atlas Mountains (Soldi 1982: 73-74). Called *ghout*, sunken fields were excavated 4 to 12 meters deep, and date trees were grown in them. It is thought that these features may have been built as early as the fourteenth century there. There is no need, however to suggest that this technology was introduced to the Andes from the Old World: there are several eyewitness accounts of the existence and use of *hoyas* on the coast of Peru at the time of the Spanish arrival (Cieza 1984 [1533]; Gasca 1979 [1553]); indeed, Cieza seems to have been quite taken with them. As Ana María Soldi points out,

> None of the chroniclers who saw the *hoyas* in the first twenty years after the European invasion expressed the least doubt that they were an indigenous system of cultivation that exploited very specific geographic conditions, and where plants were cultivated that were adapted in a very special manner to the environment created in these excavations. (Soldi 1982: 31)[3]

Other less labor-intensive means of tapping the phreatic layer were also used on the Peruvian coast. Walk-in wells were excavated down into the phreatic zone in the royal compounds at Chan Chan, in order to provide water for domestic use (Day 1974). On the south coast, to this day, when rivers cease to flow in the dry season, people excavate shallow wells several meters deep into the dry riverbeds to have access to the phreatic layer there. This practice has considerable time depth, as Cieza provides a description of this strategy being used in the Ica Valley (Cieza 1984: 221 [1533]). We have observed this strategy ourselves in use in the Nasca Valley on a variety of occasions.

In sum, not only were prehispanic coastal populations adept at manipulating river water, via canal irrigation, to provide a reliable source of water to their fields, they were also aware of the uses of groundwater. The excavation of *hoyas*, walk-in wells, and seasonal shallow wells indicates an appreciation for the utility of phreatic water, especially when or where surface water was not available. In terms of social organization, while basic canal systems could be built and maintained by individuals or small groups, large-scale irrigation—especially at the scale we see in the case of the Chimú—probably required relatively more complex sociopolitical organization not only to build and maintain the system but also to defend it and adjudicate disputes over water use. *Hoyas*, while requiring large inputs of labor for their initial construction, needed little maintenance once they were established. Likewise, walk-in wells and temporary shallow wells probably did not require large inputs of labor or complex social organization to coordinate their construction or maintenance.

In the sierra, while the lack of water was not as critical a factor as it was on the coast, it is still a fact that rainfall is limited, and irrigation is required in many areas. However, low temperatures at higher elevations had the effect of imposing an upper limit on the range of agriculture. Prehispanic populations used a variety of techniques, including manipulating groundwater, to ameliorate the temperature regime and to allow food production in otherwise inhospitable zones.

One of the major ways prehispanic people managed to overcome the effects of low temperature was to build stone-faced terraces. Terraces have higher heat storing potential than dry soil, and therefore provide relief against frost. They have the effect of raising the frost line and extending the length of the growing season at higher altitudes. Only through terrace construction was it possible to extend the range of maize agriculture through much of the sierra. In central Peru, construction of terracing on a large scale seems to have taken place during the Middle Horizon, perhaps at the behest of the Wari Empire (Schreiber 1992: 149-151). Terracing is a tremendously labor-intensive activity, but once completed the labor investment to maintain the terraces is greatly decreased. Most prehispanic terraces are still in use to this day.

Terracing has the added advantage of decreasing runoff and erosion. Rainfall will more easily soak into a horizontal surface than a sloped one, so, in effect, terracing was yet another way to manipulate and take advantage of limited water resources. Further, irrigation of terraces is more easily designed and more efficient than irrigating sloping fields.

Another example of the manipulation of water in the sierra is the case of the raised fields, called *camellones*, of the altiplano (Erickson 1985, 1986, 1987, 1988; Kolata 1986; Kolata and Ortloff 1989; Ortloff and Kolata 1989, 1993; Smith, Denevan and Hamilton 1968). In wet or inundated areas around the shore of Lake Titicaca, soil was piled up into long, narrow raised fields, leaving water channels between them. Fed by a combination of canals, derived from springs or streams, and lake water, the *camellones* were especially resistant to climatic fluctuation (Ortloff and Kolata 1993). Similar to the Wari investment in terracing, the Tiwanaku IV-V polity of the late Early Intermediate Period and the Middle Horizon may have invested substantial amounts of labor in the construction of the raised fields around the perimeter of Lake Titicaca. Like terracing, raised fields have thermal properties that raise the ambient temperature, reduce the danger of frost, and lengthen the growing season (Kolata and Ortloff 1989).

Unfortunately, the raised fields were not immune to the extended drought that began after AD 1100 (Thompson and Moseley-Thompson 1987; Thompson et al. 1985), and their failure may have contributed materially to the collapse of Tiwanaku (Ortloff and Kolata 1993). Only in recent years have some of the *camellones* been put back into production (Erickson 1988).

Also found near Lake Titicaca are features similar to the sunken fields of the coast. Called *cochas*, they are fields excavated down nearly to the phreatic zone (Flores Ochoa 1983), where the phreatic layer lies relatively close to the surface.

In this brief summary we have seen that, in a variety of situations, the prehispanic people of the Andean coast and sierra manipulated their natural environment in ways to ensure adequate food production. They built canal irrigation systems ranging from small-scale canals, to the enormous works of the Chimú. They tapped into groundwater resources using sunken fields (on both the coast and in the highlands), walk-in wells, and shallow temporary wells. In the sierra where temperature was an additional limiting factor, terracing and raised fields provided relief from frost and longer growing seasons, allowing maize production in the central sierra, and potato and quinoa production on the altiplano.

These systems were developed in response to normal conditions of aridity, limited rainfall, and low temperatures. Many of the systems also survived more extreme fluctuations in climate, such as the canal systems of the coast and the terraces of the sierra. Some of the systems were clearly associated with large-scale investment of labor and complex sociopolitical organizations: terrace building by Wari, raised field construction by Tiwanaku, and large-scale canal building by the Chimú. But even at simpler levels of social complexity, people knew their natural environment and how to overcome constraints imposed by that environment. Irrigation systems were in place at least by 1800 BC, and probably by as early as 2500 BC, built by individuals or small groups with little or no centralized control.

Cultural History of the Nasca Region

Before we turn to a discussion of puquios, we shall sketch, at least in broad brush-strokes, the cultural history of the Rio Grande de Nasca region, placing it in its general Andean cultural context (table 1.1). While we are generally concerned with the south coast of Peru, extending from the Pisco Valley south to Acarí, the events of greatest concern to us here are those that took place in the Rio Grande de Nasca drainage (figure 1.2). At times we shall single out the southern tributaries of this drainage (the Nasca, Taruga, and Las Trancas valleys), where our interpretations are based on data collected in several seasons of archaeological survey undertaken by Schreiber and her colleagues and students (Schreiber 1987, 1990, 1991; Schreiber and Isla 1995, 1998).

The south coast of Peru is perhaps best known for the Nasca culture that existed there during the Early Intermediate Period (AD 1-750). The fabulous ceramic and textile art of this culture is known throughout the world as some of the most outstanding examples of prehistoric craftsmanship. The great ceremonial center of Cahuachi, with its dozens of platform mounds and pyramids, was the ceremonial center of the Nasca culture (Silverman 1993). And the people of Nasca used the desert pampa below the Andean foothills as a giant canvas upon which to etch the famous geoglyphs called the Nasca Lines.

Less well known are the millennia of cultural developments that came before the Nasca culture, from the earliest hunter-gatherers of the Archaic Period through the Paracas culture of the Early Horizon. Also sometimes overlooked is the fact

Table 1.1 General Andean and Nasca regional chronologies.

	Southern Nasca Chronology	General Andean Relative Chronology	
AD 1500	Inca Occupation		Late Horizon
	La Tiza		Late Intermediate Period
1000	Post-Wari Collapse	3-4	Middle Horizon
	Wari Occupation	2	
	Loro	1	
	Late Nasca	7	Early Intermediate Period
500		6	
	Transitional Nasca	5	
		4	
	Early Nasca	3	
		2	
0		1	
	Montana	10	Early Horizon
	La Puntilla	8	
500 BC		Phases 1-7	
	???		Initial Period
1000			
2000	Late Archaic Period		Cotton Preceramic
2500			
3000			Preceramic Period
4000	Middle Archaic Period		
6000			
	Early Archaic Period		
8000			
	Paleoindian Period		
??			

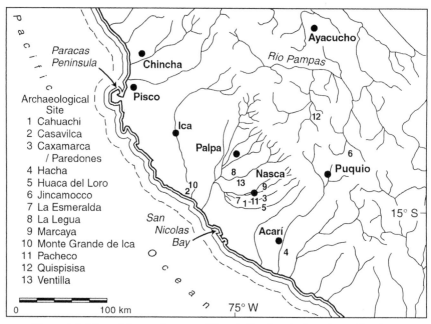

Figure 1.2 Map of the south coast of Peru indicating the locations of regions
and sites mentioned in the text.

that the Nasca culture itself underwent radical change during its history, and in fact
might better be regarded as two very different cultures, both in terms of their art
style and their social organization. And in the millennium following the demise of
the Nasca culture there is evidence of conquest by Wari, the resurgence of local
culture, and conquest again, this time by the Inca Empire.

Events prior to the emergence of the Nasca culture

The Earliest Occupations: Paleo-Indian through Middle Archaic
        The earliest people to live in the Andean region arrived in South America
perhaps as early as 13,000 years ago, during what is called the Paleo-Indian Period. Their subsistence was based primarily on hunting large mammals, as indicated by the large projectile points, such as Clovis in North America, and fishtail
points in South America, that define this period. At present we know of no occupations from this period in or around the Rio Grande de Nasca region. Sea level
was much lower at that time, so any sites that had been located along the coast are
now deep underwater.
        By 8000 BC, the climate was warmer and many of the large mammals hunted
earlier were extinct. Called the Early Archaic Period, this was a time of change to

the hunting of small mammals and collecting a variety of wild plants. Still, sea levels were lower than at present, so Early Archaic sites located along the shoreline would today be underwater. We do have evidence, however, for occupation in the sierra above the Rio Grande de Nasca area. In and near the Sondondo Valley, in the Province of Lucanas, northeast of Nasca, there are small open air sites at which have been found projectile points dating to the Puente Phase, approximately 8000-6000 BC (Schreiber 1982).

By 6000 BC, during the Middle Archaic, the Andean economy had come to be based on more intensive collecting of plants and the hunting of smaller animals in the sierra, and exploiting maritime resources on the coast, including fish, mollusks, and sea mammals. The first residents of the Nasca region that we know of at present lived there during the Middle Archaic Period. In 1952 Duncan Strong recorded aceramic shell middens along the Bay of San Nicolás, along the coastline southwest of Nasca. Published photos of lithic artifacts from that site indicate a date in the Middle Archaic (Eric White, personal communication 1995). No evidence of agricultural products was noted there by Strong (1957: 8-10).

In the Nasca Valley itself, near the core of the great ceremonial site of Cahuachi, a Middle Archaic occupation was located by Johny Isla (1990) at the site of La Esmeralda. This site was apparently a sedentary residence, complete with architecture that was remodeled through time, and a human burial. Prior to the development of agriculture, this portion of the Nasca Valley was likely wooded, and would have served as a suitable habitat for small mammals and birds that could be exploited by humans. In addition, the Nasca River flows perennially in this part of the valley, providing a good environment for wild plants and even incipient cultivation. Remains of a guinea pig were found, apparently an offering placed in the construction (Isla 1990: 75). Mollusk shells were present, indicating that marine resources also formed at least a small part of the diet, even though the site is located more than 40 kilometers from the coast.

Late Archaic (2500-1800 BC)

Often called the Cotton Preceramic, the Late Archaic was a period during which coastal subsistence was based primarily on a maritime economy (fish, sea mammals, mollusks), but during which people also grew certain industrial crops such as gourds and cotton. These products were used for domestic purposes, and for fishing nets and floats. By this time sea level had stabilized, so settlements along the coastline can be encountered today by archaeologists. Because the people were growing plants and collecting maritime resources, most major Late Archaic sites known are located in such a manner that people could exploit both the ocean and the valley bottom. That is, most sites are located along the coastline in close proximity to arable valley lands. Some of these site are quite large and exhibit the first monumental constructions in the Andean region.

Numerous sites fit this example in the Andean region, and the best known monumental sites are located mostly along the north and central coast of Peru. An abbreviated list of such sites includes Huaca Prieta in the Chicama Valley (Bird 1948), Alto Salaverry in the Moche Valley (S. Pozorski and T. Pozorski 1979), Aspero in the Supe Valley (Feldman 1987; Moseley and Willey 1973), and El Paraiso in the Chillón Valley (Moseley 1975; Quilter 1985). But on the south coast, especially in Ica and Nasca, such sites are smaller in both size and number. As we will discuss in more detail in chapter 2, the topography of these southern valleys differs substantially from that of valleys farther to the north. Unlike the valleys of the north, the arable portions of the Ica and Nasca river valleys lie well inland, far from the maritime resources necessary to support people growing cotton and gourds. We would expect to find extensive human occupation in the interior valleys of the Rio Grande de Nasca drainage only after food cultivation became the dominant form of subsistence, in the Initial Period or later. Along the coast, where the valleys are very narrow with limited arable land, we would expect to find only small Late Archaic occupations.

The site of Casavilca is a small refuse mound located on the coast one kilometer north of the mouth of the Ica Valley. At this site quantities of lithic artifacts were recovered, as well as remains of gourds and cotton (Engel 1958: 126-127). In the lowest portion of the Ica Valley, in the area called Monte Grande de Ica, Patrick Carmichael located two aceramic sites characterized by the presence of cotton (Carmichael 1991: 61-62). Carmichael located no sites dating to the Late Archaic in his survey of the coastline and lower valleys of the Rio Grande de Nasca drainage, and other surveys of the interior valleys have also failed to yield evidence of Late Archaic occupations (e.g., Browne and Baraybar 1988; Reindel and Isla 1999; Schreiber 1990, 1991; Schreiber and Isla 1995, 1998; Silverman 1993, 1994). The lack of data may indicate one of several things: that Late Archaic sites are indeed rare in the Rio Grande de Nasca region, that such early sites may now lie deeply buried, or that archaeological research has tended to focus on ceramic periods, after the development of food cultivation.

Initial Period (1800-800 BC)

During the Initial Period, major ceremonial and pilgrimage centers were built and used on the north and central coast of Peru. On the central coast these tended to have a U-shaped layout (Williams 1980); some of the major sites include Garagay and Huaca la Florida in the Rimac Valley, and Cardal and Mina Perdida in the Lurín Valley (Burger 1992: 69-75). On the north coast, ceremonial centers tended to be linear in layout with pyramids and circular sunken courts; major sites include Pampa de las Llamas-Moxeke (S. Pozorski and T. Pozorski 1987) and Sechín Alto in the Casma Valley, Caballo Muerto in the Moche Valley, and Purulén in the Zaña Valley, to name but a few (Burger 1992: 75-99). In the north highlands the Kotosh Religious Tradition took hold, and its temples have been identified at Kotosh and various other sites, including Waricoto (Burger and Salazar-Burger 1980; Burger 1992: 118-124). In the south sierra and coast, however, such complexity is not as much in evidence, although simple farming communities were numerous and widespread in the sierra.

It is a bit surprising that we have very little evidence in the Rio Grande de Nasca drainage for occupation during the Initial Period, as major occupations are known at the sites of Hacha, in the Acarí Valley to the south (Riddell and Valdez 1988), and at Erizo, in the Ica Valley to the north. Likewise, in the adjacent highland Province of Lucanas, numerous Initial Period sites have been identified, and their artifacts exhibit stylistic similarities both to Hacha and to other sites in the sierra (Schreiber 1982). Indeed, after almost two decades of systematic archaeological survey in the southern tributaries of the Rio Grande de Nasca drainage, only a single Initial Period sherd has been located. The Initial Period was a time when large-scale irrigation systems were probably first developed in other coastal valleys, but, as we shall see, large portions of the Nasca Valley were unsuitable for canal irrigation, which may explain the dearth of Initial Period sites.

La Puntilla Period (400-200 BC)

The bulk of what is usually termed the Early Horizon (800-100 BC) was a time during which the cult of Chavín became influential and widespread throughout northern and central Peru (e.g., Burger 1992). On the south coast the culture that exhibits the closest stylistic similarity to Chavín is the Paracas Culture (Tello 1959; Tello and Mejía Xesspe 1979; Engel 1966; Paul 1991). Paracas is known from the initial excavation of several major cemeteries on the Paracas Peninsula, which gave rise to the terms Paracas Necropolis and Paracas Cavernas, formerly believed to be two distinct temporal phases. (They are now thought to be roughly contemporaneous, but culturally and spatially differentiated; they both post-date the period of Chavin influence.) The most useful stylistic definition of the Early Horizon Paracas culture is that developed by Menzel, Rowe and Dawson (1964), and their phases 3 through 8 define the period during which Chavín influence is evident in the ceramic styles of Ica. During Early Horizon phase 8 the number of Paracas habitation sites increased greatly in the Ica Valley (Massey 1991; DeLeonardis 1997), and evidence of this culture spread to other valleys to the north and south.

The Puntilla Phase in the southern Nasca tributaries refers to this period of initial colonization during Early Horizon phase 8, when the first villages were founded (Van Gijseghem n.d.). Most of these villages were relatively large, suggesting a planned colonization, rather than gradual occupation by single families. Substantial settlements in the northern tributaries of the Rio Grande de Nasca drainage also occurred in phase 8 (Reindel, Isla, and Koschmieder 1999: 339-340), a period they refer to as the Späte Formativzeit (Late Formative). Silverman also documented several phase 8 sites in the Ingenio Valley (Silverman 1994: 365-368).

Montana Period (200 BC - AD 1)

Recent investigations suggest that a number of developments occurred after the end of Chavín influence but before the emergence of the Nasca culture. At this time, the apparent demise of the cult of Chavín occasioned many cultural changes throughout the Andes. In the north highlands and coast, new ceramic traditions emerged, and there is evidence of increased violence. In the Rio Grande de Nasca the local ceramic styles continued with minor change. Perhaps the most distinctive feature of this period on the south coast is the emergence of the spectacular Paracas Necropolis and Cavernas textile traditions.

What we call the Montana Period in southern Nasca includes what are traditionally defined as Early Horizon phase 10 (ceramic style Ocucaje 10) and Early Intermediate Period (EIP) phase 1 (Nasca 1). We group these phases together because of the co-occurrence of these ceramic phases at a number of sites. We find, as did Silverman (1994: 371) that ceramics of Ocucaje 10 are always found with Nasca 1 styles, although the reverse is not true: We located several single-component EIP 1 sites, and these tend to occur in defensive locations.

It appears that the Montana Period was a period of continued population growth, as the people fanned out and established new settlements throughout the region. The development of the outstanding textile art indicates perhaps the emergence of craft specialization at this time. It is likely that construction of monumental architecture at Cahuachi began by the end of this period, in EIP 1 (Orefici 1993). Indeed, the extensive cemeteries surrounding the ceremonial site include many burials with ceramics dating to Early Horizon 8 and/or 10, suggesting that use of Cahuachi may have begun earlier than EIP 1.

The EIP phase 1 defensive sites suggest an increase in conflict, as well. At the close of the Montana Period nearly every site was abandoned, and with the emergence of the Nasca culture in the next period sites were reestablished in entirely new locations.

The Nasca culture

Nasca culture pertains to the Early Intermediate Period (AD 1-750), a period during which several of the most distinctive Andean civilizations emerged. Probably the best known is the Moche culture of the north coast; others include the Lima culture on the central coast, Huarpa in the Ayacucho Basin, and various other cultures in the sierra. The chronological phases of the Early Intermediate Period are derived from the sequence of seven of the nine ceramic styles defined by Lawrence E. Dawson in the Nasca region (Nasca 1 through 9). For present purposes, Nasca 1 pertains to the Montana Period, as discussed above, and Nasca 2 through 7 pertain to the EIP Nasca culture; the last two styles fall chronologically within the following Middle Horizon.

Early Nasca (AD 1-400)

The culture that comes to mind when most people hear the word "Nasca" is what we would call Early Nasca culture, dating to EIP phases 2 through 4 (Nasca 2-4) of the Early Intermediate Period. During this period the distinctive "monumental" style of Nasca ceramics predominated (Rowe 1960). Depictions of a variety of plants, mammals, reptiles, birds, sea creatures, and supernatural beings dominate the assemblage. The designs painted on the finely made ceramics were derived from the textile art of the preceding period. In fact, the textile tradition continued into Early Nasca times, at least through EIP 2.

The great ceremonial center of Cahuachi was the apparent center of Nasca religious life. Located in the lower Nasca Valley, in what was probably sacred territory (as will be discussed in more detail below), Cahuachi was the center of an extensive mortuary cult. Cemeteries line both sides of the lower Nasca Valley for a distance of some 10 kilometers, while habitation sites of this period are rare in the lower valley. Located in the heart of this necropolis is Cahuachi, with its dozens of platform mounds and pyramids that were subject to continued enlargement and remodeling during Early Nasca times.

Excavations by Orefici (1993) and Silverman (1985, 1986, 1988, 1990, 1993) have shown that most construction at Cahuachi took place during EIP phases 2 and 3, and that in phase 4 all construction activity at the site ceased. This is taken by them to indicate that the site was abandoned in phase 4. Calibrated radiocarbon assays from samples collected by Orefici give us our best absolute dates for EIP 2 and 3: a suite of about 20 radiocarbon assays falls very tightly into the period between AD 1 and 300 (Orefici, personal communication 1990). For present purposes we tentatively extend Early Nasca to AD 400, to include phase 4.

Silverman (1990, 1993) has made a good case that Cahuachi functioned as a pilgrimage center, and that religious ceremonies were regularly held there. She sees no evidence of permanent occupation at the site. Recent excavations by Orefici have, however, turned up large amounts of habitation refuse, indicating that at least a small number of people occupied the site, probably on a permanent basis. It is clear that Cahuachi was a very special kind of site, descended from a long Andean tradition of pilgrimage centers that began as early as the Late Archaic Period on the central coast. However, we think it possible that the politicoreligious elites of Nasca society resided at Cahuachi on a permanent basis, surrounded by the symbols and trappings of power (Schreiber 1998; Vaughn 2000). Vaughn has pointed out that the high winds characteristic of Cahuachi's location would make it a favorable place for ceramic production, although no direct evidence has been found to date at Cahuachi to support this suggestion.

Silverman (1993: 324-327) argues that the site of Ventilla, in the Ingenio Valley, was a large habitation site and political center of Early Nasca society. Our observations suggest that habitation may not be as extensive as thought, and we see the site as a small ceremonial center, directly related to the pilgrimage center at Cahuachi. We have identified other small satellite centers in the Nasca and Taruga valleys as well.

Despite minor differences in opinion between the various archaeologists, all would probably agree that Early Nasca culture was relatively complex in its social and political organization, as well as in religious organization. While it certainly does not meet any definition of state-level society, this sort of society was organized at a level that anthropologists would term a chiefdom, or *cacicazgo*. There exists ample evidence for the organization and coordination of major labor projects within the Nasca sphere of influence: the construction and modification of monumental architecture at Cahuachi and its satellites, and perhaps even the construction of the geoglyphs on the nearby pampa. Such projects required the labor of large numbers of people as well as some degree of centralized control. Moreover, these projects required a level of technical sophistication, if not specialization, in fields including engineering (surveying) and architectural skills.

Early Nasca influence—as evidenced by the distribution of its ceramic style—extended north through the Ica Valley, and south perhaps to the Acarí Valley. In all valleys we find similar settlement patterns: small scattered villages with no large towns or cities (Schreiber and Lancho 1995). Excavations by Kevin Vaughn at the village site of Marcaya in the Tierras Blancas Valley indicate that villages were economically self-sufficient. He also finds evidence for differentiation of social rank, in the presence of elite households at Marcaya (Vaughn 2000).

The largest site was Cahuachi, in the lower Nasca Valley, but smaller sites with platform mounds and pyramids of the same construction style are found in several other valleys. We cannot know, based on present data, if a single ruling family or chief served the entire region in which Early Nasca culture is found, or if each valley or group of valleys had their own rulers, who in turn paid homage to a paramount chief at Cahuachi. It is likely, however, that there was some degree of elite power structure in place, and that certain individuals or groups had the power to organize large labor projects: specifically, the building and rebuilding of monumental architecture at Cahuachi and its subsidiaries.

As we will discuss in greater detail below, some people are of the opinion that the Nasca puquios were built by the Nasca culture, a term that often refers just to Early Nasca. Our data will show that the puquios probably did not exist at this time.

Transitional Nasca (AD 400-500)

It is apparent that something happened to Nasca culture sometime after AD 400, or perhaps closer to AD 500. For nearly a century it has been recognized that Nasca ceramics underwent a major stylistic change, from the "monumental" styles of Early Nasca to the "proliferous" styles of Late Nasca (Rowe 1960). Originally called Nasca A and B, respectively, the transitional style between them came to be called Nasca X (Gayton and Kroeber 1927; Kroeber 1956; Kroeber and Collier 1998). Following the seriation of Lawrence Dawson, wherein the Nasca ceramic tradition was divided into 9 styles, Nasca X corresponds roughly to Nasca 5 of his sequence, which in turn corresponds to our Transitional Nasca phase.

Not only did the ceramic art undergo a significant change, but as we have seen construction activity at Cahuachi had ceased by EIP 4. The presence of a great number of EIP 5 human burials in the region around Cahuachi suggests to us that the mortuary cult had not ceased and that Cahuachi still served as a ceremonial center. We suggest that the lack of new construction at the site does not necessarily mean that it was abandoned. Indeed, offerings from as late as the Middle Horizon have been identified at Cahuachi (Orefici, personal communication; Silverman 1987, 1993). What was abandoned was the activity involved in the remodeling and expanding of the existing mounds. It is possible that the massive labor devoted to Cahuachi in earlier times was redirected to other needs, perhaps the construction of puquios.

Settlement patterns also began to undergo some changes in this period, as old villages were abandoned and new ones established. As will be discussed in greater detail in chapter 9, recent surveys in the Rio Grande de Nasca region indicate that people began to aggregate into larger settlements in this transitional period.

Late Nasca (AD 500-750)

Late Nasca society continued the trends begun in the transitional phase. The ceramics took on a whole new look: designs became much more abstract, with an excess of "proliferous" design elements. Settlements became very large but few in number, perhaps due to new needs for defense. Data from Ica (Cook, personal communication 1994) and Acarí (Valdez 1989) indicate that a similar shift in settlement patterns was taking place in those valleys as well. Depictions of warriors on ceramics, while present in earlier phases, seem to increase in frequency. No new constructions were built at Cahuachi, but burials were still being made in the adjacent cemeteries, suggesting that it continued to serve its ceremonial functions. The Late Nasca Period remains one of the least known, but perhaps most important, chapters in the cultural history of Nasca. It appears to be a time of cultural reorganization, with perhaps more complex sociopolitical organization than in Early Nasca times.

Events following the demise of the Nasca culture

Middle Horizon/Loro Period (AD 750-1000)

Another major cultural disruption occurred at the beginning of the Middle Horizon, at which time the region was probably conquered by the Wari Empire. Wari expanded out of its core region in the Ayacucho Basin, and came to control much of the Andean sierra from Cuzco in the south to Cajamarca in the north, as well as much of the coast of Peru (Isbell and McEwan 1991; Schreiber 1992). At the same time, the old ceremonial center of Tiwanaku had established its own base of political power in the altiplano during Tiwanaku IV times, in the latter half of the Early Intermediate Period. It seems to have expanded its economic base into regions beyond the altiplano in Tiwanaku V times, in the Middle Horizon (Kolata 1993).

The Loro Period saw the establishment of a major Wari center at Pacheco in the middle Nasca Valley during what is more generally termed Middle Horizon epoch 1B (Menzel 1964), and a smaller center at Pataraya in the upper Tierras Blancas Valley in phase 2 (Schreiber 1999, 2000; Schreiber and Isla 1997). Elsewhere in the Andes, especially in the sierra and on the central coast south to Ica, Wari continued to dominate its territories until the end of phase 2 of the Middle Horizon.

Nasca social organization underwent major changes at this time (Schreiber 2000). Only recently have the local ceramic styles contemporary with the Wari occupation been identified as such. Formerly called Nasca 8, and thought to pre-date the Middle Horizon, it is now clear that the Nasca 8 style comprises the local ceramics pertaining to the Middle Horizon during the period of Wari occupation. For this reason we no longer use the numerical designation, and refer to the style and period as Loro, after the site of Huaca del Loro in the Las Trancas Valley (Strong 1957). There was a shift in the focus of settlement southward to the Las Trancas Valley, and a small local polity emerged, centered on the site of Huaca del Loro. Following the Wari demise, regional population dropped, and sites were located in hidden or defensible areas.

Late Intermediate/La Tiza Period (AD 1100-1476)

After the collapse of Wari and Tiwanaku around AD 1000 or so, and a period of cultural disruption that lasted for perhaps a century, distinctive regional cultures once again emerged throughout the Andes. Best known of these is the Chimú State of the north coast, but others include the sierra cultures of Cajamarca, the Huanca (Wanka), the Chanca, the Lupaqa, and the Colla.

Following the withdrawal of Wari, Nasca society once again continued on its own trajectory, but although it was more populous—and certainly more complex in sociopolitical terms—than it had been in the Early Intermediate Period, its ceramic art never attained the artistic heights that it reached in Early and Late Nasca times. Many new settlements, including large towns and one site of nearly urban proportions (La Tiza), were established. Population apparently expanded greatly, and part or all of the Rio Grande de Nasca region was probably ruled from La Tiza, in the Nasca Valley. Excavations at Pajonal Alto in the Taruga Valley by Christina Conlee indicate that this was a period of ever-increasing economic interaction (Conlee 2000).

Inca Conquest and Occupation (AD 1476-1533)

Beginning in the mid-fifteenth century, the Incas in the south highlands of Peru began a series of conquests that was to culminate in the largest empire known in the New World. From their capital at Cuzco they conquered the entire Andean region from Ecuador to Chile, including the sierra and much of the coast. They apparently took control of the south coast in about AD 1476, and in Nasca met with little resistance (Menzel 1959). They established a center at Caxamarca (today called Paredones) in the Nasca Valley, and another at La Legua in the Ingenio Valley.

At present the evidence suggests that few changes were wrought in the Nasca

region as a result of the Inca occupation, and, given the existence of local central-
ization, it seems likely that the Incas left rule in the hands of the local elites (cf.
Menzel 1959). Caxamarca/Paredones, rather than being administrative in nature,
may actually have been a private retreat belonging to one of the Inca emperors
(Schreiber 1993). The coastal Inca road passed through the region, crossing the
desert from the lower Ica Valley, past the area of the confluence of the northern
Nasca tributaries, arriving at the Inca center at La Legua, in the Ingenio Valley.
The road then continued through the lower portions of the southern valleys (see
discussion in chapter 2).

Colonial Period (1533-1824)

In 1533 the Inca ruler, Atahuallpa, was killed by Pizarro, and the Spanish
proceeded to take control of the former empire. Our earliest records for Nasca
indicate that it was ruled by a man named Don Francisco Nanasca, and the Spanish
used his name to refer to the region; its proper name was probably Cajamarca. The
Jesuits eventually acquired large landholdings in the area, specifically in the Ingenio
Valley, land originally sold by Nanasca in 1546 (Cushner 1980: 17). That valley
came to be known for the wine-producing grapes grown there.[4]

Notes

1. The term *puquio* has a variety of meanings in Quechua, all of which have in common the denoting of a source of water. Most commonly used to refer to a natural spring,
puquio can also refer to man-made water sources, such as sunken fields, irrigation canals,
and filtration galleries. Because the aqueducts of Nasca are called puquios by the people
who use them, we shall follow their lead and continue the use of this term here. It has
become fashionable in some circles to use the word *acueductos* to refer to them, in part to
try to pique the interest of tourists. It is also sometimes the case that European terms are
privileged over indigenous ones reflecting a feeling that European terms are more scientific
and therefore more appropriate.

2. From this point forward we shall no longer italicize the word "puquio" when referring to the puquios of Nasca.

3. Original text: "Ninguno de los cronistas que vieron las hoyas en los primeros veinte
años después de la invasión europea expresó la menor duda de que se tratara de un sistema
de cultivo indígena que explotaba condiciones geográficas muy peculiares y donde se
cultivaba plantas indígenas que se adaptaban de manera muy especial al ambiente creado
dentro de las excavaciones."

4. It should be noted that many references to Nasca in colonial documents are referring
to the larger region, not specifically to the town or valley of Nasca. Indeed, many of the
documents use Nasca when referring to the Ingenio Valley, which had a substantial Spanish
occupation.

CHAPTER 2

THE NATURAL ENVIRONMENT AND HYDROLOGY OF NASCA: THE PROBLEM OF THE LACK OF WATER

While today Nasca is a verdant paradise, and has been so for some time, the physical environment in which it is located would seem to present almost insurmountable obstacles to human occupation. There is essentially no rainfall on the south coast of Peru, owing to a combination of cold offshore ocean currents and other climatic conditions, and in most years Nasca receives no measurable rainfall. Moreover, the rivers of Nasca are deficient in water, and they can hardly be counted on to provide relief from the lack of rain. The lack of water in Nasca is most severe. But the very conditions that limit life in Nasca are the very ones that set the stage for the construction of the puquios, so here we turn to a discussion of those conditions. Specifically, we shall consider the geological setting of Nasca in general, and the hydrological conditions of the Nasca, Taruga, and Las Trancas valleys in particular.

The Rio Grande de Nasca drainage is formed of a series of river valleys and usually dry washes that flow out of the Andes and through a single channel to the Pacific Ocean (figure 2.1). The major rivers, from north to south, include Santa Cruz, Grande, Palpa, Viscas, Ingenio, Nasca, Taruga, and Las Trancas. While most Andean rivers flow directly to the sea, in the Nasca region the trajectory of the rivers is blocked by a series of coastal hills. These coastal hills are the eroded remains of an ancient range of mountains predating the Andes. The region is relatively active, tectonically, and is crisscrossed by small faults (Montoya et al. 1993).

Geologically, the character of the region was created by the emergence of the Andean batholith, which formed the basement structure of the Andes Mountains. As this batholith arose, it heated and deformed the existing rock strata, producing an overburden of metamorphic rocks, rich in metals and minerals. The many small gold mines in the Nasca region are a testament to this process. Volcanic activity in

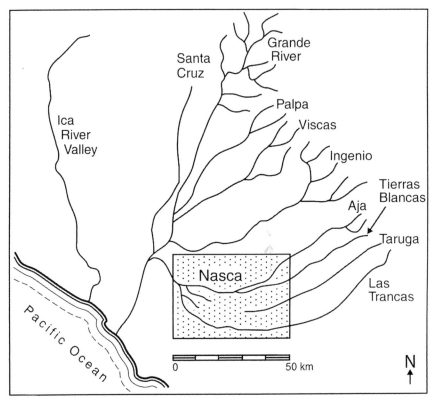

Figure 2.1 Map of the south coast of Peru showing the various tributaries of the Rio Grande de Nasca drainage. The southern tributaries, the primary focus of this study, are highlighted.

the young Andes produced the thick basalt flows that cap the mountains in this region, resulting in broad flat puna lands, ideal for camelid grazing. Indeed, the Pampa Galeras vicuña preserve is located in the Province of Lucanas, Ayacucho, just above Nasca. Volcanic activity also produced a large deposit of ash that covers the western flanks of the Andes, above the southern tributaries of the Rio Grande de Nasca.

The terrain created between the coastal hills, underlain by the older San Nicolas batholith, and the Andes is a broad flat plain (pampa), well known today as the location of the Nasca geoglyphs: the lines and ground drawings. Originally a shallow bay, this desert pampa now lies 400 to 500 meters above sea level, and the sandy soil is covered by a continuous scatter of small reddish-brown stones. The geoglyphs were created by moving those small stones to the side, leaving an open path exposing the lighter colored soil below. The main portion of the pampa, that with the best-known figures, lies south of the Ingenio Valley and north of the Nasca Valley, but numerous geoglyphs are found south to the Las Trancas Valley, and north to the Grande, as well.

In the basin created between the Andes and the coast range, another set of phenomena created unique conditions in the region. The rising coastline has exposed large deposits of sand. At the same time a variety of factors produce severe winds, locally called *paracas*, that blow through the region, distributing the sand from south to north. The southern flank of the middle Las Trancas Valley is almost completely covered by barchan dunes and a large moving sand sheet, and sand is beginning to cover the north flank of the valley as well. As the sand has covered over archaeological sites dating to as late as the Late Intermediate Period, the encroachment of the sand sheet on the Las Trancas Valley may have occurred only in the last millennium or so. Large dune fields are common from Acarí in the south to Ica in the north. Perhaps the most distinctive topographic feature on the south coast is the sand-covered mountain that towers over the Nasca Valley, called Cerro Blanco (figure 2.2). This is one of several sacred peaks in the region, along with Tunga (also called Huaricangana), the highest point along the coast range, Cerro Illacata near the Pampa Galeras, Oscconta, a basalt formation just north of the Pampa Galeras, and Qarwarazu, an extinct volcano on the puna to the northeast (Reinhard 1986).

According to local beliefs, each of these mountains is home to a mountain deity, called *apu* or *huamani*. The *huamani* of Cerro Blanco is female, while the other four are male, and several play a role in the various versions of the myth that

Figure 2.2 Cerro Blanco as viewed from the Nasca Valley. (Photo by Jim Wheeler.)

explains the origin of Cerro Blanco. She was said to be beautiful and young, and the wife of either Illacata or Qarwarazu, depending on the version of the myth. One day while her husband was sleeping, she ran off with handsome young Tunga. When her husband awoke and realized she was gone, he became furious and chased after the errant couple, creating storms and earthquakes as he went. Frightened, Tunga hid the young woman under a pile of white corn pollen, and himself nearby under a pile of blue corn pollen. There they remain to this day: Cerro Blanco, the beautiful maiden, and Cerro Azul at her side, her eternal suitor.

Cerro Blanco is believed to be the source of the water in all the puquios, as will be discussed below. Each year offerings are made on its summit to ensure the rising of the waters in the puquios (Reinhard 1986).

Nasca Hydrology

Returning to our discussion of the natural setting, the existence of the coastal range, besides delimiting the pampa, also had the effect of cutting off direct access to the Pacific of the rivers flowing west-southwest out of the Andes. As a result, the rivers all join the Grande River, and flow out through a single pass in the coastal hills. We can conveniently divide the Rio Grande de Nasca drainage into two groups of tributaries. The northern group includes the Santa Cruz, Grande, Palpa, Viscas, and Ingenio rivers; of these, the Santa Cruz flows only intermittently, while the Grande has the greatest volume of water. The southern group includes the Aja, Tierras Blancas, Taruga, and Las Trancas rivers; the Aja and Tierras Blancas join (via three separate channels) to form the Nasca River. In turn, the Nasca, Taruga and Las Trancas rivers all join to form a single channel and flow northward some distance before they join the Grande.

As a result of this unusual arrangement of Andean foothills, desert pampa, and coastal hills, most arable land, and thus most human occupation, is located some distance inland from the Pacific. For example, the modern town of Nasca lies 60 kilometers from the Pacific, as the condor flies, at an elevation of 600 meters above sea level. A similar situation holds in the Ica Valley, the next drainage north of Nasca; it, too, is nestled behind the coast range, and most occupation is found well inland. In contrast, most coastal Peruvian valleys are characterized by broad expanses of arable land nearest their lowest extremes, on the large alluvial fans formed near the Pacific. Cities such as Lima and Trujillo were established very near the coastline. In Nasca, not only is the best arable land located far inland, but the valleys are narrow, resulting in very limited agricultural land capable of supporting human populations.

We can also see that the Rio Grande de Nasca rivers vary greatly in average annual volume (figure 2.3). The northern tributaries (Santa Cruz, Grande, Palpa, Viscas, and Ingenio), which have normal dendritic drainage patterns, have much higher volumes of water than the southern tributaries (Aja, Tierras Blancas, Taruga, and Las Trancas), with the exception of the Santa Cruz River. In terms of average monthly flow, we can see that the southern tributaries have much lower flow, even in the peak months of February and March, and they cease to flow entirely during the months of June through October (table 2.1; figure 2.4). If we look closely at a map of the southern tributaries we notice two things that differentiate them from the northern tributaries. First, their overall catchments are relatively small, owing to the fact that the Acarí river's catchment extends around and behind them (figure 2.5). Second, these rivers flow in very straight courses down the western slopes of the Andes, with few tributaries. The surface soil on these slopes includes high quantities of volcanic ash, which is very porous and absorbs much of the rainfall that it receives. As can be seen, the actual runoff collected in the southern tributaries is very low compared to the size of their catchments (table 2.2); this is a direct reflection of the high rate of infiltration in those drainages. Thus the southern tributaries not only have smaller catchments than the northern tributaries but they also collect less runoff from the Andean rains, owing to the volcanic soils. The low volume in turn contributes to even higher rates of infiltration. It should be noted as well that the ONERN measurements in the southern tributaries were taken at higher elevations, between 625 and 850 meters above sea level, where river discharge should be higher; in the northern tributaries all measurements were taken at or below 500 meters above sea level.

As a case in point, the Aja River, which has the greatest volume of the four southern tributaries, has an average annual volume of only 30.27 million cubic meters of water, compared to 198.05 million cubic meters of water that flow down the Grande River (ONERN 1971). Further, the Aja River receives only 92,387 cubic meters of water per square kilometer of its catchment, as compared with 164,725 cubic meters per square kilometer reaching the Rio Grande. The rivers of the Rio Grande de Nasca drainage, in turn, pale in comparison with other coastal valleys (figure 2.6), such as

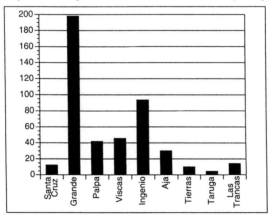

Figure 2.3 Average annual discharge of the rivers of the Río Grande de Nasca drainage, in millions of cubic meters per year. The northern tributaries, with the exception of Santa Cruz, have higher discharge than the southern tributaries.

Table 2.1 Average monthly flow of the rivers of the Río Grande de Nasca drainage, in cubic meters per second. As can been seen, none of the southern tributaries have any water flowing in them at any time from June through October, while two of the northern tributaries flow all year round, on average. (Source: ONERN 1971: 2: 42-51; based on observations taken 1947-1968.)

RIVER	Jan	Feb	Mar	Apr	May	Jun	Jul	Aug	Sept	Oct	Nov	Dec
Santa Cruz	0.46	2.25	1.81	0.32	0	0	0	0	0	0	0	0
Río Grande	9.37	28.8	28.3	7.14	1.37	0.46	0.27	0.19	0.2	0.11	0.12	0.61
Palpa	1.46	6.79	6.17	1.59	0.26	0	0	0	0	0	0	0.12
Viscas	1.86	7.69	6.46	1.41	0.22	0.01	0	0	0	0	0	0.18
Ingenio	5.19	12.3	13.6	3.77	0.42	0.08	0.05	0.05	0.04	0.04	0.06	0.59
Aja	2.67	4.22	3.67	1.02	0.09	0	0	0	0	0	0.01	0.12
Tierras Blancas	0.72	1.53	1.45	0.16	0.01	0	0	0	0	0	0	0.01
Taruga	0.3	0.71	0.62	0.08	0	0	0	0	0	0	0	0.01
La Trancas	1.29	1.86	1.98	0.33	0	0	0	0	0	0	0	0.01

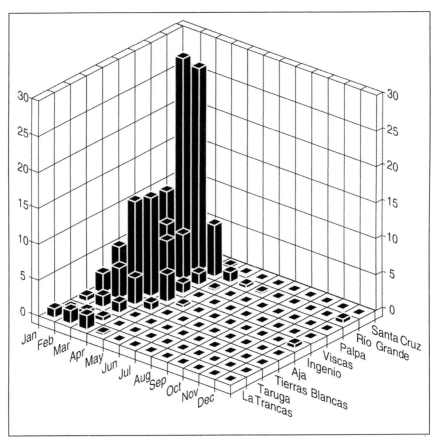

Figure 2.4 Average monthly discharge of the rivers of the Río Grande de Nasca drainage, in millions of cubic meters.

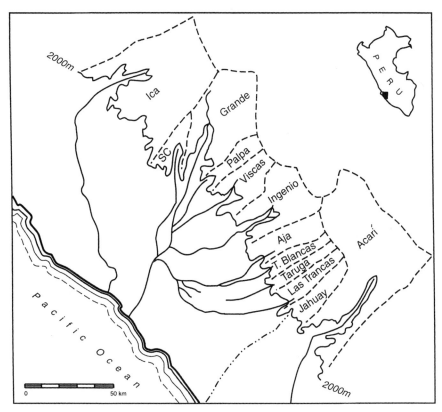

Figure 2.5 Map of catchments of rivers from Ica to Acarí. The southern tributaries of the Río Grande de Nasca have exceptionally small catchments due in part to the extension of the Acarí drainage to the east in the sierra.

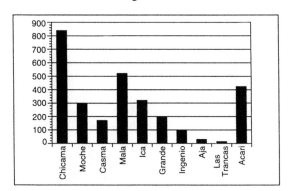

Figure 2.6 Average annual discharge of selected rivers along the coast of Peru, from Chicama on the north coast to Acarí in the south. The rivers of the Rio Grande de Nasca drainage have extremely low annual discharge when compared to other rivers of the coast.

Table 2.2 Average annual discharge of the rivers of the Río Grande de Nasca drainage (in millions of cubic meters per year) relative to the size of their catchments (in square kilometers). The southern tributaries not only have catchments that are smaller than those of the northern tributaries, with the exception of Santa Cruz, but the amount of water remaining on the surface is lower, relative to the size of the catchment. This is an indication of the higher rates of infiltration characteristic of the southern tributaries. (Source: ONERN 1971, Vol. 2: 42-51; based on observations taken 1947-1968.)

RIVER	elevation	discharge (x)	catchment (y)	x/y
Santa Cruz	600	12.3	169	0.0728
Río Grande	425	198	1202	0.1647
Palpa	375	41.9	286	0.1465
Viscas	425	45.7	528	0.0866
Palpa-Viscas		87.5	814	0.1075
Ingenio	500	93.7	846	0.1108
Aja	750	30.3	328	0.0924
Tierras Blancas	850	10.1	288	0.0351
Taruga	625	4.4	156	0.0282
La Trancas	725	14.2	280	0.0507

the Chicama Valley (839.43 million cubic meters) of the north coast (ONERN 1973). Further, as will be demonstrated below, the water flow statistics for the southern tributaries are misleadingly high.

Fed by seasonal precipitation in the Andes Mountains, at elevations above about 2000 meters above sea level (m asl), the catchments of the southern Nasca tributaries are substantially smaller than those of the northern tributaries, as we have seen, and very small in comparison to other coastal valleys, thus accounting for the low initial river volume in the southern valleys. These southern tributaries flow down the western flanks of the Andes, until they reach the deep alluvial valley bottom in the lower foothills. This alluvium has a moderate to high infiltration capacity; the infiltration of water into the alluvium results in a substantial transmission loss in river volume, especially at elevations below 1200 m asl. Thus these rivers are what are termed "influent streams," meaning that they flow partially on the surface, and for some stretches drop completely below the surface. Below the surface the water continues to flow downward toward the sea; this subsurface water is properly termed the phreatic layer.

The initial point at which the rivers drop below the surface varies from valley to valley, depending on water volume, and varies within each valley seasonally and annually. In years of good rainfall in the adjacent highlands, the rivers will flow continuously along their length. Once rainfall ceases in the highlands, the volume of river water decreases, eventually reaching the point where it can no longer flow on the surface, but will filter into the alluvium, and flow underground. The critical limiting factor is the point at which the water disappears below the surface in the dry months (May through January) of the year. In years of good rainfall this point will be located farther downstream than after years of drought. As we have observed, for example, highland rainfall was quite substantial in the first several months of 1989, and the Aja/Nasca River was through-flowing during the months of February and March. When the highland rains ceased, the river volume dropped, and the river gradually ceased to flow on the surface in the middle valley. In September 1989, after a half year of dry weather in the highlands, we observed that the Aja River reached only to an elevation of 800 meters above sea level, about 9 kilometers upstream of the modern town of Nasca, before dropping below the surface. In 1990 the rains were poor, and in September of that year the river was flowing only to an elevation of 900 meters above sea level, three kilometers farther upstream than the previous year. In 1991 after a second year of drought, the river reached only to an elevation of 1,050 meters above sea level, another three kilometers up from the previous year. That year the Tierras Blancas River, which has lower initial volume than the Aja River, flowed only to an elevation of 1,500 meters above sea level, some 23 kilometers upstream of the modern town of Nasca. Local informants and our own observations indicate that the rivers are through-flowing only two years out of seven, on average. Thus, in most years the middle portions of the southern valleys are devoid of surface water for the entire year.

In sum, the point at which the rivers disappear beneath the surface of the riverbed will be closer to the middle valley in years of good rainfall, but progressively farther away after years of drought. In the middle valley, under natural conditions, there is no water available to irrigate the agricultural fields in years of low highland rainfall—five years out of seven. Further, there is no water available for domestic uses in the middle valley. Only by tapping the phreatic layer is life possible in this zone.

Recent research by Donald Proulx, David Johnson, and a team of geologists from the University of Massachusetts indicates that the phreatic layer in the middle valleys is supplemented by water directed into it by a series of geological faults (Johnson et al. 2002). These faults are sometimes aligned with impervious rock outcrops on the valley flanks. Thus the phreatic layer is most productive under or adjacent to the dry river courses, and in some places along the valley sides where faults may direct subsurface water into the valleys.

Moving farther downstream, the rivers reemerge at the surface once again. In the Nasca Valley, at an elevation of about 400 meters above sea level, the river reappears suddenly on the surface and continues to flow. Interestingly enough, and in contrast to the location where the river disappears initially, it seems that the point of reemergence does not vary, either seasonally or after prolonged droughts. The Nasca River emerges at a place called Las Cañas, located some 15 kilometers west of the town of Nasca. Each time that we have observed it, over the past fifteen years, the river has emerged at exactly this point. Aerial photographs from both 1970 and 1944 show it emerging at this point. Maps, both current and older, indicate that the river begins to flow at this point. Archaeological remains also indicate that the river probably appeared at this point in antiquity: it is exactly at this point that large ceremonial mounds and extensive cemeteries appear along the valley flanks, continuing westward and including the great ceremonial center of Cahuachi. The emergence of water at this point was almost certainly regarded as sacred in prehispanic times.

From this point on, the stream is perennial for a distance of about 9 kilometers, passing through Cahuachi, Estaquería, and Tambo de Perro, to its confluence with the Taruga and Las Trancas rivers. From there the stream variously appears and disappears on the surface, passing through the region called Jumana, until its confluence with the Grande River.

The Las Trancas River also reemerges at about 400 m asl, in the region called Tunga. Local informants say that the point of emergence varies less than a kilometer from year to year. The smaller Taruga River emerges in at least two separate quebradas, to a point at or just below the surface, again like the other valleys at en elevation of about 400 m asl. The emergence of the water in a consistent location in each of these valleys serves to explain the route of the ancient road that passes through the region, probably used by the Incas as one of their royal roads, and historically called the Camino Leguía. This road takes the form of a geoglyph for much of its course, which is not surprising considering that many of the lines probably did serve simply as roads. Silverman (1993: 324-325) has argued that this road served to connect Cahuachi with the site of Ventilla in the Ingenio Valley, across the pampa, and that its route was determined by symbolic factors. We observe that, while the road does connect the two valleys, it does not lead directly to either site but rather enters the valleys about 1.5 kilometers from each site. We suggest that there may be a more pragmatic explanation for the route taken by this road: it was designed to lead the traveler to reliable sources of water. The road exits from the Ingenio Valley at a natural break in the valley wall, the same place that the modern road emerges—one of very few natural exits out of that entrenched valley. It then follows a perfectly straight course across the pampa to a natural point of ingress into the Nasca Valley, and intersects it at a point three kilometers downstream of the point where the river reemerges. One can always find water at this location. Likewise, as the road continues on to the south, it intersects Atarco and Carrizales, the points at which the Taruga River appears at the surface, and Tunga, the point at which the Las Trancas River reemerges on the surface. If travelers wished to pass through the southern Nasca region in such a way to guarantee themselves access to drinking water, this ancient road is exactly the route one would take.

Valley Subdivisions

For present purposes, each of the southern valleys may be divided into five sections, based on availability of surface water (figure 2.7). The elevations given here are based on the Nasca-Aja Valley, and may vary slightly in other valleys.

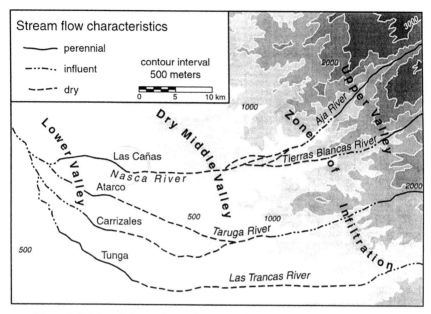

Figure 2.7 Map of the southern tributaries of the Río Grande de Nasca showing their division into five zones: sierra and upper valley, where river flow is perennial; the zone of infiltration, where water is sometimes present on the surface; the dry middle valley in which puquios are used to tap the phreatic layer; and the low valley in which the rivers are once again perennial, at least for a distance.

(1) *Sierra*: above 2,000 m asl. Rainfall farming is possible, generally on terraced valley sides.

(2) *Upper Valley*: between 1,200 and 2,000 m asl. Water is usually available year-round flowing in the river. Valley bottom agriculture is practiced, using river water for irrigation.

(3) *Zone of Infiltration*: between 800 and 1,200 m asl. This is a transitional zone between the upper and middle valleys. Water is available most years, but this zone may gradually dry up in years of prolonged drought. Valley bottom agriculture is practiced, using usually available river water for irrigation.

(4) *Middle Valley*: between 400 and 800 m asl. This zone is devoid of surface water except during times of flood, which occurs roughly two years out of seven, generally in February and March. At other times no surface water is available for either irrigation or domestic uses. The largest expanse of valley bottom arable occurs in this sector of the valley. The system of puquios was developed to tap the phreatic layer to provide water and enable occupation of this zone.

(5) *Lower Valley*: below 400 m asl. The river reemerges on the surface, and flows perennially for a distance of some 9 kilometers; thence, it is influent until its confluence with the Grande River. Valley bottom agriculture possible with river water irrigation. Severe winds and heat inhibit occupation of this zone.

The distribution of surface water has two profound effects on human occupation. First, the rivers cannot be relied upon to provide irrigation water every year in the dry middle portion of the valley. Irrigation canals can (and do) draw water from the river flowing higher up in the valley, but the volume of water is so low that at present such canals extend a maximum of only one to two kilometers. The problem is further compounded by the fact that the lower reach of the rivers is constantly changing. Permanent intakes would have to be built far up-valley to guarantee a supply of water in all years, making the cost of such an undertaking prohibitively high for the low volume of water that would result. Large, long distance canals simply do not occur in these valleys, and there is no evidence for their having existed in the past. The only possible major irrigation work that we have seen is the partial canalization of one of the natural watercourses, called the *riachuelo,* which connects the Aja and Tierras Blancas rivers along the north flank of the La Puntilla ridge. In this way, water from the higher volume Aja River could be diverted into the lower volume Tierras Blancas River in times of flood.

River-based irrigation agriculture in the broad middle valleys is therefore limited to years of flood, roughly two years out of seven. On the other hand, land in the upper and lower valleys is arable year-round due to perennial stream flow. Unfortunately, while the arable portion of the middle valley is generally 2-3 kilometers wide, the lower valley narrows to less than 1/2 kilometer, and the upper valley is even narrower. Thus most of the arable land in Nasca lies in the portion of the valley lacking surface water for irrigation.

The second profound effect that the lack of water has on human occupation is the fact that there is no water available for domestic uses in the dry middle valley. This zone is therefore poorly suited for human habitation except during periods of flood. During the dry season and during periods of drought the phreatic layer is too deep (about 10m deep in the central portion of the valley) to be conveniently tapped by wells. However, at the upper and lower extent of the middle valley the aquifer is shallower, and domestic water can be drawn from shallow wells dug in the dry river bed. As we discussed above, this is common practice in Nasca as well as in other valleys with influent streams. In contrast to the middle valley, the upper and lower valleys do have available year-round supplies of water for domestic purposes.

The Problem

How were the ancient peoples of Nasca to cope with these conditions and solve the problem of the lack of water? At first they might choose to live only in the upper and lower portions of the valley, those zones in which the river could be relied upon for both irrigation and domestic water. But if population grew beyond the capacity of those very limited areas, what were the people to do? Worse, what if a serious drought in the highlands reduced their already meager supply of river water?

The people could have responded in one of two ways. First, they could have simply moved away. If there were too many people to be supported, then the excess would have to move to a new location, in some other valley. Or, second, they could develop a new source of water. They could find a way to tap the water in the phreatic layer and bring its water to the surface where it could support human occupation. In this way they could open up the middle valley for occupation. As we shall see, this is exactly what they did.

CHAPTER 3

PUQUIOS:
THE SOLUTION TO THE PROBLEM

How does one go about tapping the phreatic layer in such a way as to be able to use the water for irrigation? One might excavate a deep well, but without a level of technology that includes such things as water wheels or pumps, how could the large quantities of water necessary for irrigation reach the fields? Certainly one might excavate large walk-in wells, such as the Chimú did at Chan Chan, but these provide only a bucket or pot of water at a time, and they suffice only for domestic purposes. What is needed is a way to tap water deep beneath the ground, and use gravity alone to bring it to the surface in large quantities.

Thus we are presented with a seeming conundrum: how to move subsurface water to the surface by running it downhill. But when we consider the fact that the surface of the land is not flat, that it slopes gently downward from east to west, from the Andean foothills to the Pacific Ocean, a solution presents itself. For example, at a specific point on the surface, say in the place called Cantalloq, the phreatic layer lies 10 meters below the surface. However, some distance west of Cantalloq is a point at which the surface of the land lies at a lower absolute elevation than the phreatic layer at Cantalloq. If that point on the surface to the west can be connected with the phreatic layer beneath Cantalloq to the east, subsurface water will be brought to the surface by running it downhill.

The simplest means to accomplish this is to connect the two points with an open trench. The trench will be 10 meters deep at Cantalloq, and get gradually shallower as the land drops in elevation but the trench stays nearly horizontal, sloping downward only enough to keep the water flowing. At the point at which the trench reaches the surface of the land the water can be stored in a *kocha*—a reservoir—or it can flow directly into the system of irrigation canals. Most of the puquios were originally constructed in this manner, as open trenches. Alternatively, a tunnel may be bored through the earth connecting the point on the surface with the phreatic layer to the east. A number of puquios have segments or branches that were constructed as tunnels rather than open trenches. Tunneling is a much more difficult and dangerous process, as the tunnel must be shored up as it is dug

35

through the loose soil and gravel of the alluvial valley bottom. The resulting galleries are lined with stones, but without mortar so water can filter in between the
stones; stone slabs or wood beams form the ceiling. A number of formerly open
trenches have since been partially filled, leaving tunnel-like galleries at the base of
the former trench through which the water continues to filter.

Puquio Function and Construction

A puquio is thus a horizontal well: an open trench and/or a subterranean gallery
that connects a point on the surface with subsurface water. The underground water
filters into the puquio, flows through it, and empties into either a small reservoir
(*kocha*) or directly into irrigation canals. Puquios provide not only a reliable source
of irrigation water but also a year-round supply of domestic water.

At present twenty-nine puquios water land lying between the elevations of
450 and 675 meters above sea level in the Nasca Valley, a horizontal distance of
some 16 kilometers, extending from Soisonguito to Orcona. In the Taruga Valley
there are today only two puquios functioning, and they water a small expanse of
land, just two kilometers long, lying between 550 and 600 meters above sea level.
In the Las Trancas Valley there are five functioning puquios that water land between 525 and 675 meters above sea level, from Chauchilla to Totoral, a horizontal distance of 11 kilometers. So to the best of our knowledge, there are a total of
thirty-six puquios still functioning in these three valleys. Some puquios have been
substantially altered since the Spanish conquest, and a number of puquios have
been abandoned or destroyed. The original number and distribution of puquios
was certainly greater, and we are certain that there were at least thirty puquios in
the Nasca Valley, three in the Taruga Valley and eight in the Las Trancas Valley, for
a total of forty-one. And there is evidence that their number may have been even
higher, as will be discussed in more detail in chapters 4 through 8.

Each puquio is named. Usually it is called to by the name of the tract of land
it waters (not the land through which it flows), although sometimes the name of an
individual who lives nearby will be used to refer to the puquio. Names can change
through time, although most puquios seem to have kept the same names for at least
the last seventy years. About one-fourth have Spanish names, such as Agua Santa
or Conventillo, but the majority carry indigenous names, such as Ocongalla, Orcona,
or Cantalloq. Some puquios have multiple branches that are named separately,
such as Achaco, whose branches are called El Grande and El Chico, but in each
case a single name refers to all branches that share a single reservoir.

While a number of puquios are simply open trenches (figure 3.1a), most com-
bine different construction techniques (table 3.1): in many cases the upper portion
of the trench has been filled, creating a subterranean gallery (figure 3.1b), while
some have been extended in length by tunneling (figure 3.1c). Several puquios
have multiple branches, and different branches may employ different combina-

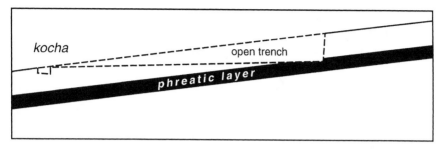

Figure 3.1a Diagram of an open trench-type puquio.

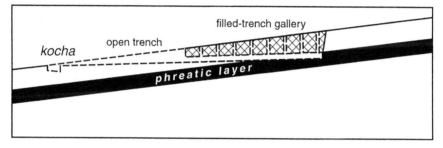

Figure 3.1b Diagram of a puquio with filled-trench gallery.

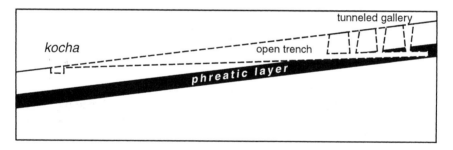

Figure 3.1c Diagram of a puquio with a tunneled extension.

tions of construction techniques. Additional very short branches, called *cangregeras* (from the Spanish word for crab), may extend off the sides or end of a puquio, to increase the quantity of water filtering into it.

Puquios that are open trenches their entire length tend to be the shorter, shallower puquios. The base of the trench is usually only a meter or so wide, but the trenches widen to 10 meters or more at the surface, taking up quite a bit of surface land. Large berms are found along the sides of such puquios, parallel to the course of the trench, the result of the excavation of the trench, and the cleaning of wind-blown silt and other material out of the trench during periodic cleanings. The sides of the trench are usually lined with river cobbles that form retaining walls

Table 3.1 Puquio construction types. Under comments we note, in the case of puquios with tunneled sections (extensions of the main trench, or added branches), where the tunneled section reaches.

Irrigation Sector	Puquio	open trench	filled-trench gallery	tunnel extension	tunnel branch	comment
Nasca	Soisongo	X				
	Soisonguito	X				
	Conventillo	X				
	Agua Santa	X				
	Ocongalla	X				
Aja	Llicuas Norte	X	X		X	to riverbed
	Llicuas Sur	X	X			
	San Marcelo	X	X			
	La Joya de Achaco	X				
	Achaco	X				
	Anglia	X	X	X		to riverbed
	Curve	X				
	Cuncumayo	X				
	Aja Norte	X				
	Aja Sur	X		X		to riverbed
	Aja Alto	X				
	Bisambra	X	X		?	under river
	Huachuca	X	X	X		under river
	Tejeje	X	X			
	Cortez	X	X			
	Vijuna	X	X			
	Orcona	X	X	?	?	under river
Tierras Blancas	Majoro	X	X		X	under river
	Majorito	X				
	Huayrona	X	X	X		
	San Antonio	X		?		
	Pangaraví	X	X			
	Kallanal	?	?	?		under river
	La Gobernadora	X	X	X		toward river
	Santo Cristo	X	X			
	Cantalloq	X		X	X	under river
Taruga	Santa Maria	X	X			
	San Carlos	X	X			
	Camotal	X				
Las Trancas	Chauchilla	X	X			
	La Joya	X	?			to riverbed
	Kopara	X	X			
	El Pino	X	X			
	Pampón	X	X			
	Huaquilla	X				
	Totoral	X	X			
	Huayurí	X	X			under river

that are stepped back, much like terraces. Trench retaining walls are repaired annually and thus change slightly in configuration from year to year. We therefore have not tried to systematically record trench reinforcing for each puquio, except to note in general any exceptions to the usual forms. Trench type puquios sometimes have multiple branches, as in the cases of Aja Norte and Achaco (figure 3.2), but more commonly are simple, single channel puquios.

In the case of longer, deeper puquios much of the trench may have been filled in, as discussed above, to create what we refer to as "filled-trench galleries." Such filling of trenches reclaims substantial tracts of land for agriculture by reducing the surface area taken up by open trenches. Some of the longer and deeper puquios also have segments built by tunneling beyond the upper end of the trench; we will refer to these as "tunneled galleries" to distinguish them from the former.

The opening of either type of gallery into a puquio trench appears as a tunnel, much like a mineshaft (*socavón*), out of which water is freely flowing (figure 3.3). The sides of a gallery are typically faced with river cobbles and broken stones fit together without mortar. Water filters into the gallery through the interstices between the stones. The ceiling of the gallery is sometimes made of dressed stone slabs, and sometimes made of wood beams, usually huarango (*Prosopis chilensis*), which is said to be very durable. However, wood does not preserve forever, so each time a gallery is cleaned, the beams that are beginning to rot or be worn away by the action of flowing water are removed and replaced with new beams. While we have rarely attempted to enter the galleries of the puquios ourselves, we do

Figure 3.2 Oblique aerial photograph of the puquio Achaco, an open trench-type puquio.

Figure 3.3 The opening from the gallery into the open trench of the puquio Cantalloq.

have eyewitness accounts of the interiors of a number of them, and base our data on those observations. In specific cases, these eyewitness accounts are included in our descriptions of the puquios, in chapters 4 through 8.

While we have never observed a prepared floor surface in any puquio, and neither have our informants reported any, earlier writers report that a gallery might be lined with wood or stone to prevent erosion (Rossel Castro 1977: 172). According to González García (1934: 208), and repeated by later writers, some galleries were excavated through hard conglomerate and had no need of facing stones along their sides; we, on the contrary, have never observed a gallery without stone sides, nor have any been reported by informants. The dimensions of the galleries that we have seen fall in the range of about 60-80 cm wide and 80-100 cm high, in the case of tunneled galleries. Filled-trench galleries vary widely in size, and some are said to be so tall that a person can walk upright through the gallery.

Spaced along the galleries at varying intervals are *respiraderos*, also called *chimeneas*, or, more commonly, *ojos*. These are holes dug between the ground surface and to the gallery to provide a means of access into the galleries during the annual cleaning (figures 3.4 and 3.5), and to let in air and light. The form and dimensions of the *ojos* also vary according to the manner of construction of the individual galleries, as will be discussed in more detail below.

Our mapping of the puquios relied on the presence of *ojos* visible on the surface to indicate the subterranean path of the galleries and any major branches (figure 3.6). We have been told that some galleries have short side feeder branches without *ojos*, but we cannot observe these branches from the surface. A comparison of our observations with the reliable ones made by González García (1934), and with aerial photos taken in 1944, indicates that there are many more *ojos* today than there were in the past. New *ojos* are typically built when a cave-in has blocked the flow of water through a gallery; it is much safer to dig a new *ojo* than to clear the obstruction from inside the gallery. (For one example, see the discussion of the puquio Cantalloq in chapter 6.)

In the case of some puquios we have observed that the *ojos* are very large, very deep, and conical in profile; these are typical in the case of galleries that were built by tunneling. Roughly circular in form, these *ojos* can have a diameter at the surface of the ground as big as 15 meters, while at their base they narrow to about a meter where they provide access into the galleries. Usually such *ojos* are closed at the bottom to prevent soil or other materials from falling into the galleries and blocking them. We rarely observed such *ojos* to be open, and many had a meter or more of accumulated soil and vegetation, making exact measurement of their depth impossible. These large *ojos* are spaced a few tens of meters apart, and they may have irregular stone-faced retaining walls, stepped back much like terraces. In general no large berms parallel the course of these puquios. In most of these cases it is apparent that the gallery below was originally built as a tunnel. Some of the *ojos* may have been built at the time of construction, but many were added more

Figure 3.4 The gallery of the puquio Aja Sur visible at the base of an *ojo*, 8 meters below the surface of the land. The water can be seen flowing through the gallery.

recently, as can be seen by comparing older and more recent aerial photographs.

In other cases we observe that the *ojos* are small and square, and lined with wood. These *ojos* are generally 60 to 80 centimeters wide, and the sides are formed of cribbed wood beams with stone cobbles places in the interstices (figure 3.7). These *ojos* tend to be more closely spaced, only a few meters apart. It is usually the case that there are the remains of berms parallel to the course of a puquio with small *ojos*, and that the ground over the course of the puquio may be slumped down somewhat (figure 3.8). In such cases it is clear that the puquio was originally excavated as an open trench, and at some later date the gallery structure was built in place, the cribbed *ojos* built, and then the trench refilled with soil. The remaining berms result from the excess soil not refilled into the trench, and slumping has occurred due to the settling of the fill as it compresses over time.

We cannot know with any precision whether a trench was filled immediately after the original construction of the puquio, or later. Local informants state that they were filled within the past century and, given their current state of preservation, this seems not unlikely. Open-trench puquios are inconvenient barriers to the distribution of irrigation water on the surface, and they take up much potentially arable land, so there is good reason to fill them in. Unfortunately, when this filling

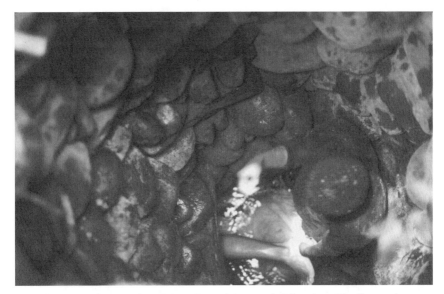

Figure 3.5 The cleaning of the gallery of the puquio Bisambra. The first worker stands in the bottom of the *ojo,* while the second, whose lower leg is visible, enters the gallery and clears it of silt and debris. The material is collected in plastic rice sacks and passed to the first worker, who in turn passes it to workers on the surface.

Figure 3.6 Lines of *ojos* of the puquio Majoro visible as round holes in agricultural fields.

Figure 3.7 Small square *ojo* of cribbed wood, from the puquio Huayrona.

took place, in many cases the ceilings of the tunnels and the walls of the *ojos* were made of wood (figure 3.9). While this might have been an expedient measure at the time of filling, within a few decades or so the wood deteriorates and must be replaced. Trees are a very limited resource at present, so the filled-trench sections of the puquios are in the poorest state of preservation. It is impractical to replace the great quantities of wood they contain, so as sections fall in they are left open (figure 3.10). For example, in 1934 González García described the puquio Agua Santa as including a long segment of gallery that was in a bad state of repair; this puquio is at present an open trench its entire length, indicating that the fill was simply removed sometime after he observed it.

By considering the types of *ojos* present, the presence or absence of lateral berms, and the degree of slumping over a subterranean gallery, we are able to distinguish between tunneled galleries and filled-trench galleries, especially where the surface of the land has not been altered too extensively. In some cases we have found that inspection of aerial photographs from 1944 reveals details of construction no longer in evidence. In our original documentation of the puquios we did not systematically consider this aspect of construction, and we have most recently revisited and restudied each puquio to ascertain more precisely its construction type. As we shall discuss below, the distinction between filled-trench galleries and tunneled galleries may have some bearing on the history of the puquios and the dating of their construction.

The most recent innovation in trench filling can be seen in the cases of the Kopara and Chauchilla puquios of the Las Trancas Valley, and Santo Cristo in the

Figure 3.8 Filled-trench type gallery of the puquio Santa Maria. The slumping of the fill over the gallery, in the original trench, can be seen clearly. Three of the men are standing next to small, cribbed *ojos*, spaced only a few meters apart.

Figure 3.9 Wood lintels from a section of filled-trench gallery of the puquio Pampón. In this case the fill over the gallery has been washed away or has fallen in, exposing the wooden lintels.

Figure 3.10 The puquio La Gobernadora with open trench at the upper right, filled-trench gallery in the middle section, and tunneled gallery in the lower left. Note that portions of the filled-trench gallery have fallen in and been left open.

Nasca Valley. In these cases cement tubes were laid as conduits for the water in the bottoms of the trenches, vertical cement tubes were spaced about every 50 meters to provide access from the surface, and the trenches were filled in, at some time after 1944. These puquios are visible (or nearly invisible, actually) on the surface only as a line of widely spaced cement-lined wells, each less than 1 meter in diameter (figure 3.11).

The depth of each puquio is of course determined by the depth of the aquifer. Puquios are shallower at the upper and lower extent of their range, because the phreatic layer is closer to the surface, and deepest in the middle section where the phreatic layer is deepest. Some shallower puquios lie along the valley sides, where they may tap water directed into the valley by geological faults (Johnson et al. 2002). The length of a puquio is determined by two factors, the depth of the aquifer and the slope of the land: the deeper the phreatic layer, the longer the puquio; the shallower the water, the shorter the puquio. By the same token, the steeper the slope of the surface, the shorter the puquio; the more gradual the slope of the land, the longer the puquio must be.

Puquio output is related to the location of the individual puquio, and the source of its water (table 3.2). The puquios with the highest output tend to be those located immediately next to the riverbed, especially those with galleries that extend up to or under it. It seems that the river water that has filtered beneath the surface of the land, while probably fanning out as far as the impervious sides of the valley, is higher in concentration immediately beneath the normally dry riverbeds.

Figure 3.11 Small cement *ojos* in the upper portion of the puquio Santo Cristo.

Table 3.2 Puquio locations relative to water sources. Most puquios are located adjacent to riverbeds, while a small number begin up against the valley sides; others are located out in the flat valley bottom, close to neither the riverbeds nor the valley sides.

Valley	Puquio	river	valley center	valley side
Nasca	Soisongo	X		
	Soisonguito	X		
	Conventillo		X	
	Agua Santa	X		
	Ocongalla	X		
Aja	Llicuas Norte	X		
	Llicuas Sur		X	
	San Marcelo		X	
	La Joya de Achaco		X	
	Achaco			X
	Anglia	X		
	Curve			X
	Cuncumayo	X		
	Aja Norte			X
	Aja Sur	X		
	Aja Alto		X	
	Bisambra	X		
	Huachuca	X		
	Tejeje	X		
	Cortez	X		
	Vijuna	X		
	Orcona	X		X
Tierras Blancas	Majoro	X		
	Majorito	X		
	Huayrona	X		
	San Antonio		X	
	Pangaraví		X	
	Kallanal			
	La Gobernadora		X	
	Santo Cristo			X
	Cantalloq	X		
Taruga	Santa Maria	X		
	San Carlos		X	
	Camotal		X	
Las Trancas	Chauchilla	X		
	La Joya	X		
	Copara		X	
	El Pino	X		
	Pampón	X		X
	Huaquilla		X	
	Totoral			X
	Huayurí	X		

Other puquios with high output are located along the valley margin alongside impervious rock outcrops that extend into the valley, possibly consistent with the presence of faults. These outcrops may also cause a sort of damming effect of the river-derived phreatic layer, and it is notable in this regard that the puquios always tap subsurface filtrations on the upstream side of the outcrops. On the other hand, puquios located out in the valley bottom, away from either the riverbeds or the valley sides, tend to have lower output than others.

Recently Johnson et al. have argued that the water in the puquios is derived from a series of geological faults that direct subsurface water into the valley from the north or south (Johnson et al. 2002: 310). In the case of those puquios that are located along the valley margin, we suspect they are correct. For example, in the area of Aja, the two branches of Aja Norte and the small puquio, Aja Alto, are located away from the river, and they may tap subsurface water that comes from an independent source (see Johnson et al. 2002: 319-322). Indeed, the close proximity of three puquio sources suggests this is a region especially rich in filtrations. (We note, however, that the southern branch of Aja, Aja Sur, which derives its water from under the dry riverbed, produces a greater volume of water than Aja Norte.) A similar situation holds in the case of the puquio Achaco, which has three, and possibly four, branches tapping sources of water near the impervious valley edge, away from the river. This is the only puquio that did not dry up in the extreme drought of 1860-1864 (see chapter 5, below). The puquio Orcona has three branches, two of which follow the trajectory of the riverbed, but the third of which begins up against the valley side. Johnson et al. have documented the location of another major fault, probably directing water to this latter branch of the puquio (2002: 322-324). Other puquios that would bear closer scrutiny include Curve, located between Aja and Achaco, Santo Cristo, on the south side of the Nasca Valley, the shorter branch of Pampón, in the Las Trancas Valley, and the puquio Totoral, also in Las Trancas.

We continue to maintain, however, that the majority of the puquios derive their water from the subterranean flow of the rivers, and they are ultimately fed by seasonal rainfall in the sierra. In a normal year, the rainy season begins in December in the sierra, and within a few days or weeks water flows down the rivers toward the Nasca region. Whether or not the rivers are through-flowing or drop underground depends on the volume of water they carry. The volume of water in the rivers each month (see table 2.1 and figure 2.4) is a direct result of highland rainfall, and a relative measure of that rainfall. The rivers begin to rise in late December, increase in volume in January, and reach their maximum flow in February and March. The flow then drops off in April, and by May the rivers are mostly dry.

If we compare the seasonal flow of the rivers with the number of puquios functioning each month (table 3.3), and the total volume of water emanating from them (table 3.4), we see that the water in the puquios rises in March or April, roughly two to three months after the rivers flow, and they continue to produce good amounts of water until June or July, two to three months after the rivers begin

Table 3.3 Number of puquios with measurable output, by month, 1985-1994.

	1985	1986	1987	1988	1989	1990	1991	1992	1993*	1994
January**								10	5	2
February								9	5	2
March	31	32	28	31	22	16	18	8	6	10
April	31	32	26	31	31	22	26	15	32	36
May	32	32	25	30	32	22	27	15	33	36
June	31	32	20	30	32	16	25	14	33	37
July	32	32	16	29	31	14	21	19	27	36
August	30	31	10	23	26	7	21	20	20	29
September	25	26	8	20	20	7	18	23	15	22
October	25	23	8	17	16	7	15	25	10	17
November	18	19	7	15	12	4	13	22	2	16
December	15	14	6	10	9	4	11	21	2	12

*prior to 1993, only 33 puquios were measured; in 1993 this number increased to 37
** due to extremely low output, puquios were not measured in January and February until 1992

Table 3.4 Total puquio output (in millions of cubic meters), by month, 1985-1994.

	1985	1986	1987	1988	1989	1990	1991	1992	1993*	1994
January**								0.3	0.1	0.1
February								0.2	0.1	0.1
March	4.7	3.8	2.1	2.4	1.2	0.6	0.7	0.2	0.2	0.3
April	5.3	4.2	1.5	2.3	2	1.1	1.5	0.4	1.3	2.9
May	4.1	4.3	1.3	2.1	2.7	1	1.4	0.4	1.8	3
June	3.5	3.9	0.9	1.8	2.4	0.7	1.1	0.4	1.6	2.5
July	3	3.1	0.7	1.5	2.2	0.5	0.8	0.4	1.1	2.4
August	2.5	2.6	0.4	1.2	1.7	0.3	0.8	0.5	0.7	1.3
September	1.6	1.7	0.3	0.9	1.1	0.2	0.5	0.5	0.5	0.9
October	1.3	1.3	0.3	0.7	0.8	0.2	0.5	0.6	0.3	0.6
November	0.7	1	0.2	0.5	0.5	0.1	0.4	0.6	0.1	0.6
December	0.4	0.6	0.1	0.3	0.3	0.1	0.3	0.5	0.1	0.4

*prior to 1993, only 33 puquios were measured; in 1993 this number increased to 37
** due to extremely low output, puquios were not measured in January and February until 1992

to dry up. Their highest output occurs in April or May, again just two to three months after the rivers peak. The precise correlation between the cycle of rainfall/ river flow and the rise and fall of the water in the puquios, is clear evidence that the majority of the puquios capture the underground filtrations of the rivers.

To bolster their argument that the puquios tap an independent source of water, Johnson et al. assert that "the filtration galleries, which are located throughout the Nazca Valley, *always flow continuously* even when other wells which [sic] tap the subterranean water in the river gravels have long since failed" (Johnson et al. 2002: 310; emphasis added). We see quite clearly from the data presented in table 3.3 that most puquios function seasonally, and that many do dry up in the months of the austral summer. For example, in 1985 and 1986, years with exceptionally high puquio output, nearly all puquios were functioning in March through August, but fewer than half of the puquios had measurable flow in December. The worst year in the sequence, 1990, shows only two-thirds of the puquios functioning in April and May, and only four (of 33) with measurable output in December. While a handful of puquios always seems to flow, it is incorrect to claim that all of them flow continuously. The few puquios not susceptible to the seasonal availability of river water may include the small number of puquios that derive their water from the geological faults described by Johnson et al.

(We draw the reader's attention to the anomalous data from the year 1992, when more puquios functioned in the second half of the year, and when their output, while very low overall, was higher in those months as well. That year was a year in which an ENSO (El Niño) event disrupted climatic patterns, and had severe and lingering effects in Nasca.)

Most puquios have small reservoirs, *kochas*, at their lower end from which waters are directed into irrigation canals (*acequias*). More than any other puquio feature, *kochas* seem to be in a constant state of renovation: out-takes may be refitted with cement slabs and wooden sluice gates; some *kochas* have been enlarged and lined with cement; others have had their sides raised, increasing their capacity, but submerging the lower portions of their trenches. Only a few *kochas* remain unimproved (figure 3.12)

There is a modern version of the puquio, called the *pozo-kocha*, that is still

Figure 3.12   An unimproved *kocha,* at the puquio Aja Alto, in need of cleaning. Standing on its banks are author Prof. Josué Lancho and local resident Otto Pflucker.

actively constructed in this region. In areas where the aquifer is not too deep, typically near the upper and lower ranges of the distribution of the puquios, a deep straight trench is excavated down to the aquifer with heavy machinery (figure 3.13). Water filters into the *pozo-kocha*, and it is then extracted with motor-driven pumps. Some former puquios have been transformed into *pozo-kochas*. In these cases the lower end of the puquio is destroyed and the portion of the puquio that intersects the aquifer is left open; this also serves to increase valuable arable land. Such alteration is most common in the Las Trancas Valley, where at least three puquios (Huaquilla, Huayurí, and one branch of El Pino) have been converted. At least one puquio in the Nasca Valley (Soisongo) has also been converted into a *pozo-kocha*.

Figure 3.13 The excavation of a *pozo-kocha* in the Las Trancas Valley.

History of Research

The puquios of Nasca are mentioned in historic documents written at least as early as 1605. Many travelers and visitors noted their existence and commented upon them, and they are mentioned in various legal documents. The first scientific mention of the puquios of which we are aware was made by Alfred Kroeber in 1926, who wrote in his field notes: "It was said that twenty-eight puquios had been located and cleaned out in the past year (1925) on the hacienda Taruga" (Kroeber and Collier 1998: 83). (By "puquios" he was referring to the series of what he called wells, or what we know as *ojos*.)

In 1927 Toribio Mejía Xesspe was working as research assistant to Dr. Julio C. Tello in the Nasca region, and took the opportunity to investigate several puquios; he published his observations in 1939. He provides a description of six puquios in the Las Trancas Valley and one in the Taruga Valley; he lists, but does not describe, eight puquios in the Nasca Valley (Mejía Xesspe 1939).

In 1934 the Consejo Superior de Aguas commissioned a study of the puquios by the engineer M. Francisco González García. His report, or at least part of it, was published that year by the Directorate of Waters and Irrigation (González García 1934). In 1978 that article was reprinted, making it accessible to the archaeological community (González García 1978). However, the reprinted version of the article contains minor editorial errors, such as omitting some decimal points, and several important features were omitted from the redrafted version of González García's map, including several puquios.

González García's study is the most complete and accurate treatment of the puquios to date in the Nasca Valley, and we rely on his observations to provide comparisons with our own and to document changes in the puquios between 1934 and the present. The version of the report published in 1934 does not include descriptions of puquios in the Taruga or Las Trancas valleys, although we have reason to believe that those other valleys were also included in his study. A later writer, Rossel Castro, apparently had a copy of the original report, and he used it quite extensively in his own descriptions of the puquios (1942; 1977). For example, in the published version of González García's report there are profile diagrams of five puquios: Achaco, Bisambra, Huachuca, Vijuna, and Majoro. Rossel Castro's 1977 chapter includes these same five diagrams, plus four more: Aja, Pangaraví, and Cantalloq in the Nasca Valley, and Pampón in the Las Trancas Valley. So we can be sure that González García studied at least one puquio in the Las Trancas Valley, and we think it not unlikely that he was as thorough there as elsewhere. Unfortunately, however, we are limited to the data in his published article, as we have not been able to locate the original report.

It is also clear that other writers used the data of González García, and not always with direct attribution. There were two puquios in the Nasca Valley that González García did not describe, possibly because they were of minor importance, or perhaps they were so badly maintained that they were not functioning in 1934. These puquios, La Joya de Achaco and Santo Cristo, are also absent from the writings of those who relied on González García.

Interestingly, González García noted at the beginning of his report that "[d]isgracefully, not all of the puquios that they built have been preserved. There are many that have been destroyed and only vestiges are found of others" (González García 1934: 207). And it is clear that even more have been destroyed since his time. We may never know what their original number was.

Alberto Regal took great interest in the technological innovations of prehispanic Andean cultures, publishing summary works on such topics as Inca roads and bridges (e.g., Regal 1936). In 1943 he published a table summarizing the descriptions and measurements of the puquios in the Nasca Valley. Most of his data were taken directly from González García's article: nearly all measurements are exactly the same, he uses precisely the same names, and he is missing the same two puquios, La Joya de Achaco and Santo Cristo. However, Regal did provide some measurements that González García did not, indicating that he did actually observe some of the puquios himself.

Alberto Rossel Castro was a priest who lived in Nasca between 1941 and 1950, and who apparently took a great interest in local archaeology, including the puquios. In 1942 he published an article about the puquios; in his 1977 book on the archaeology of the south coast of Peru he included a chapter on the puquios that essentially replicates the 1942 article, with only minor differences. Rossel Castro was not a trained scientist, and the inconsistencies in his reports can cause a measure of frustration to the careful reader. At first we tended to disregard much of what he wrote because of these inconsistencies, but we have come to have great respect for his dedication and for his efforts to understand the puquios. While his data are sometimes unreliable, it is clear that he did personally observe many of the puquios, and he is perhaps the only researcher who crawled through several of them; these observations are invaluable.

In 1960, a University of Tokyo expedition conducted a study of irrigation systems in coastal Peru; their report includes a discussion of the puquios in the Nasca Valley, and a reproduction of González García's diagrams and the map (omitting only minor details in this case) (Kobori 1960: 83).

In 1986-1987 the Peruvian development agency, CORDEICA, sponsored a study of the puquios, directed by the engineer Felix Solar La Cruz (CORDEICA 1987), and later published by him (Solar 1997). This project accomplished the cleaning of nine puquios and the detailed mapping of five.

The Present Study

Our ongoing collaboration in the study of the puquios began in 1985 (Schreiber and Lancho 1988, 1995). Lancho is a lifetime resident of Nasca and he is the acknowledged local expert on the puquios. In 1986 he conducted a survey of the puquios for the Consejo Nacional de Ciencia y Tecnología (CONCYTEC) (Lancho 1986). That same year Schreiber undertook a project designed to document and map all the existing puquios, and she began to look at the archaeological setting in which they occur (Schreiber 1987). The authors have made additional observations of the puquios between 1986 and the present.[1] Since 1986 Schreiber has undertaken several seasons of systematic archaeological settlement survey in the Nasca, Taruga, and Las Trancas valleys (Schreiber 1987, 1990, 1991; Schreiber and Isla 1995, 1998). These surveys have documented archaeological remains directly associated with the puquios and evidence of shifts in settlement patterns correlated with the construction and use of the puquios.

Extensive use has been made of aerial photography in our studies, as the puquios are most clearly viewed from above, in their natural and cultural context. The earliest photos covering the entire region, available from the Peruvian Air Force National Aerial Photography Service (SAN), were taken in 1944. These photos enable us to corroborate (or correct) the descriptions presented by Mejía Xesspe, González García, and Rossel Castro. In addition, the 1944 photos provide invaluable data regarding puquios that have been destroyed or altered since that date; they also provide clues to the existence of puquios that had already fallen out of use by 1944, but whose traces were still visible. The second set of SAN aerial

photographs that we used was taken in 1970; these provide a good contrast with
the photos of 1944, enabling us to pin down the date of certain alterations to the
quarter century that separates those two dates. In our descriptions of the puquios,
below, we will frequently draw contrasts between conditions in 1944 and 1970,
based on these two sets of photos. Schreiber has also photographed the puquios
from the air on numerous occasions, since 1986, providing color photographs of
the puquios in their current state.

In the following chapters we present descriptions of each of the functioning
puquios as well as evidence for the existence of puquios now lost or destroyed.
We structure our presentation according to the division of the region into "Irrigation Sectors" by the Peruvian Ministerio de Agricultura (figure 3.14). We devote
one chapter to each of these sectors.

(1) The Nasca Irrigation Sector is located in the Nasca Valley, below the
confluence of the Aja and Tierras Blancas rivers. In this sector are found four

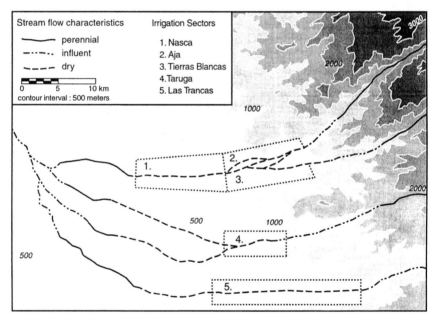

Figure 3.14 Map of the southern Nasca region indicating locations of
irrigation sectors.

puquios, one former puquio, and a possible lost puquio.

(2) The Aja Irrigation Sector extends across the northern half of the Nasca Valley, from the confluence of the Aja River with the Tierras Blancas River up into the lower Andean foothills; it includes lands lying north of the Tierras Blancas River. In this sector are found sixteen puquios, plus one or more possible lost puquios.

(3) The Tierras Blancas Irrigation Sector extends across the southern portion of the Nasca Valley, including those puquios located to the south of the Tierras Blancas River. It extends from just east of the confluence with the Aja River up to the beginning of the Andean foothills. In this sector are found nine puquios, plus one possible lost puquio.

(4) The Taruga Irrigation Sector lies in the central portion of the Taruga Valley, to the south of Nasca.

(5) The Las Trancas Irrigation Sector lies in the Las Trancas Valley, the southernmost tributary of the Rio Grande de Nasca drainage.

Puquio Descriptions

We summarize, in table 3.5, some basic puquio data.

(1) The location of each puquio is given in Universal Transverse Mercator (UTM, Zone 18) coordinates. In each case the coordinates indicate the location of the *kocha*, or else the point at which the puquio enters the system of acequias if there is no *kocha*. (These coordinates were estimated from topographic maps of the region; at the time of our field study handheld GPS receivers were not available.)

(2) The length of each puquio is noted, given as the measurement (in meters) from the *kocha* to the end of the longest branch. (More details are provided in the verbal description of each puquio in the following chapters.)

(3) The depth of the puquio indicates the depth (in meters) below the current ground surface of the filtrations captured by the puquio. While measuring the depth of open-trench puquios was a relatively simple matter, galleries posed a different problem, especially if their *ojos* were closed. We measured the distance (in meters) from the surface of the ground to the top of the water level in the gallery at the base of every open *ojo*, in 1986. In the case of large conical *ojos*, which might have a diameter of 10 meters or more at the surface, we strung a rope from one side of the *ojo* to the other, directly over the open gallery. The weighted end of a flexible 50 meter measuring tape was tossed over the rope, and lowered vertically into the *ojo*, until it touched the water in the gallery. The intersection of the rope and the measuring tape provided the depth of the *ojo*. In most cases we were not able to measure the depth of the uppermost (and deepest) *ojo*, so some puquios may be slightly deeper than the measurement we provide here.

(4) The storage capacity of each *kocha* is given in cubic meters. These data

Table 3.5 General puquio data.

Sector	Puquio	UTM: Easting	Northing	max length (m)	depth (m)	kocha (m3)	output (lps)	terrain (ha)	families	1970 photo 175-70-	1944 photo 524-
Nasca	Soisongo	497200	8360450	n/a	4	n/a	35	65	1	2460	686
	Soisonguito	498200	8630600	597	5	350	25	98	2	2449	666
	Conventillo	499500	8360600	559	6	510	25	74	1	2448	665
	Agua Santa	499700	8360100	552	6	320	35	84	6	2448	665
	Ocongalla	500800	8359800	592	6	350	30	56	4	2447	664
Aja	Llicuas Norte	503400	8360600	608	5	200	20	23	8	2444	662
	Llicuas Sur	503650	8360250	472	5	240	25	27	1	2444	662
	San Marcelo	504200	8360350	433	6	none	20	20	10	2443	661
	La Joya de Achaco	502450	8360600	260	4	no data	10	no data	4	2445	663
	Achaco Norte	503050	8361700	648	5	3000	50*	249	25	2467	662
	Achaco Sur	"	"	1024	5	"	"	"	"	"	"
	Anglia	504150	8361400	591	5	320	30	77	1	2443	661
	Curve	504350	8362050	541	10	550	30	75	16	2468	660
	Cuncumayo	505700	8361700	537	7	n/a	20	51	9	2441	659
	Aja Norte	506400	8362100	658	8	350	70*	160	37	2440	658
	Aja Sur	"	"	775+	9	"	"	"	"	"	"
	Aja Alto	507100	8362350	246	4	200	no data	12	6	2440	658
	Bisambra	507700	8361350	1069	7	810	50	140	36	2440	673
	Huachuca	508050	8361450	791	8	430	35	62	17	2439	672
	Tejeje	509450	8361600	521	6	300	35	93	3	2438	671
	Cortez	510400	8361800	301	5	160	30	19	8	2437	671
	Vijuna	510750	8361850	389	6	none	25	31	17	2436	670
	Orcona	511200	8362200	1080	5	320	50	148	41	2436	669

Sector	Puquio	UTM: Easting	Northing	max length (m)	depth (m)	kocha (m3)	output (lps)	terrain (ha)	families	1970 photo 175-70-	1944 photo 524-
Tierras Blancas	Majoro	503100	8359300	1249	7	960	35	116	17	2404	677
	Majorito	503800	8359250	823	6	250	30	125	14	2405	677
	Huayrona	504500	8359400	842+	7	220	20	123	29	2405	676
	San Antonio	505050	8359500	510	6	600	15	54	5	2406	676
	Pangaraví	506250	8359800	761	6	1000	20	109	5	2407	674
	Kallanal	506300	8360350	no data	no data	none	15	39	7	2407	674
	La Gobernadora	507550	8360250	676	8	150	30	86	16	2408	673
	Santo Cristo	509100	8360560	521	7	350	20	15	13	2410	672
	Cantalloq	509550	8361200	471	10	300	50	157	18	2410	671
Taruga	Santa María	508600	8351950	644	10	350	25	40	2	2580	999
	San Carlos	509450	8351350	391	8	380	20	12	6	2561	998
	Camotal	507450	8351900	425	n/a	n/a	n/a	n/a	n/a	2579	1000
Las Trancas	Chauchilla	509300	8344400	1280	no data	no data	no data	no data	no data	2612	904
	La Joya	511200	8344300	~900	n/a	n/a	n/a	n/a	n/a	2614	878
	Kopara	512500	8344700	~750	no data	800	50	no data	14	2616	877
	El Pino	514250	8344700	920	7	450	40	30	18	2617	875
	Pampón	515150	8344850	1480	6	none	35	77	6	2618	874
	Huaquilla	516700	8345100	~500	n/a	n/a	n/a	n/a	n/a	2620	873
	Totoral	518000	8344000	654	8	1200	25	20	4	2621	872
	Huayurí	520550	8344600	?	n/a	n/a	n/a	n/a	n/a	2623	870

* this measurement represents the sum of all branches

were provided by the Junta de Usuarios in Nasca.

(5) The maximum output of each puquio is given in liters of water per second, as measured in May 1994. These data were provided by the Junta de Usuarios in Nasca. 1994 was a year of average puquio output (totaling about 15 million cubic meters), and the month of May was the month of peak puquio output that year. Although puquio output varies from year to year, not to mention seasonally, these data provide a measure of the relative productivity of each of the puquios. We note in our discussions of individual puquios cases where poor maintenance of the puquio may be a factor contributing to lower than expected flow. If the reader compares current output measurements to those recorded by González García, the reader will find that current volume seems to be much higher; this can be partly explained by the fact that González García made his measurements in the months of August and September, a time when puquio output is low and dropping.

(6) The terrain watered by each puquio is expressed in hectares. Again, these data were provided by the Junta de Usuarios in Nasca.

(7) The number of families served by each puquio was recorded in 1995. If one compares present data to those collected by González García, it will be noticed that the current number of users is generally higher today than in 1934. In 1934 many of the puquios served individual haciendas, or large *fundos*. Since the breaking up of the large landholdings in the agrarian reforms of the late 1960s, more individual families control lands and puquio water now than in the past.

(8) Finally, we include the catalog numbers of aerial photographs with the best views of each puquio, available from the Servicio Aerofotográfico Nacional (SAN) in Lima, Peru. Those from 1970 were taken in the month of March, and some intermittent water flow is visible in the rivers. The project number is 175; so the full catalog number for the photo of Soisongo would be 175-70-2460. The 1944 photos were taken in the month of December, the driest time of year; each individual photo number is preceded by 524, the project number.

Our discussion of each puquio begins with the location of the puquio relative to the natural landscape, and its distance from the modern town of Nasca, as measured from the Plaza de Armas to the *kocha*. Where necessary, we include other names used for the puquios, as well as alternate spellings where these are sufficiently different from our spelling that they might cause confusion (e.g., Curve vs. Kurpe). Each puquio is described, including manner of construction and measurements of each section given. We shall proceed in each case beginning at the *kocha*, and working our way upstream to the point(s) of origins of the puquio. While this may strike the reader as counterintuitive (and we agree that it is), all prior descriptions of the puquios (except Schreiber and Lancho 1995) proceed in this manner. Therefore, by following the same sequence, our data can more easily be compared to data collected by González García and those who followed in his footsteps. In those cases where significant changes have taken place since the puquios were recorded in 1934 and the present, we discuss those differences and the reasons for them; we will often draw on comparisons of aerial photographs from 1944 with those taken in 1970 and/or our own observations. Associated archaeological sites or artifacts will be discussed where they are present. And in those cases where local legends or oral traditions pertain to a particular puquio, we summarize them as well. Finally, we present the meaning of each puquio name, where these are known.

Notes

1. The data and interpretations reported herein should be regarded as our most current assessments, and supersede all documents we have written or published in the past. Even since publication of our most recent article in *Latin American Antiquity* (Schreiber and Lancho 1995) we have continued to observe the puquios and update our records. The careful reader will note that we have been able to document additional side branches of some puquios, or greater length of others, as new observations are reported to us by those who clean the galleries. And we shall continue to collect new data as they become available.

CHAPTER 4

PUQUIOS OF THE NASCA IRRIGATION SECTOR

There are presently four puquios (Soisonguito, Conventillo, Agua Santa, and Ocongalla) functioning in the lower Nasca Valley, plus a fifth (Soisongo) that has been converted into a *pozo-kocha* (figure 4.1). Below this point there is a large tract of land that may have been watered in times past by a now lost puquio (Ayapana). In general, puquios in this irrigation sector have good to high output, indicating an abundance of filtrations in the sector. These puquios are also relatively shallow, given that the phreatic

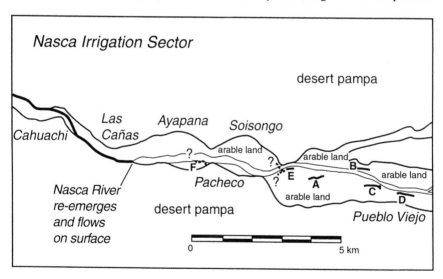

Figure 4.1 Map of the Nasca Irrigation Sector showing limits of arable land, riverbeds, and locations of current and former puquios: A. Soisonguito; B. Conventillo; C. Agua Santa; D. Ocongalla; E. Soisongo; F. Ayapana. Dashed lines indicate the portion of a puquio that has been destroyed or converted; if the puquio today functions as a *pozo-kocha*, this portion of the feature is indicated with a solid line.

layer lies closer to the surface than it does in the middle valley. Only 6 kilometers
downstream from the location of the former Soisongo puquio, at Las Cañas, the phreatic
layer intersects the surface of the riverbed, and the river flows perennially from this
point, down past Cahuachi, and on to Tambo de Perro.

Soisonguito

Soisonguito is a trench-type puquio located just south of the Nasca riverbed, 9
kilometers west of Nasca (figures 4.2 and 4.3); it has a *kocha*. It captures filtrations very near the riverbed, and angles slightly away from the riverbed toward the
southwest, and measures 597 meters from its *kocha* to its point of origin. In this
case, and in the case of all trench type puquios, our measurements of its length can
be taken as complete, since the zone of filtration is clear. The phreatic layer lies
about 5 meters below the surface of the land at this location.

The puquio is flanked by a large berm on its north side and a smaller berm on
its south side. As we will see in the case of a number of puquios, the large berms
created by the initial construction of the puquio trenches and their subsequent cleaning are not always arranged symmetrically along both sides of a puquio. It is
usually the case that the larger berm sits on the side of a puquio trench that is
nearest the riverbed. This serves to protect the integrity of the puquio structure in
the case of any episode of river flooding, which, while rare, can be very destruc-
tive (see discussion of Orcona, in chapter 5).

Berms also provided raised surfaces that, while unsuitable for cultivation, were
suitable for small occupations, perhaps of a temporary nature while people were
planting and harvesting the adjacent fields. In the case of several puquios, including Soisonguito, there are prehistoric artifacts on and in the puquio berm; in this
case there are numerous Middle Horizon 3-4 and Late Intermediate Period artifacts on the north berm. Such artifacts can be explained as either (1) the remains

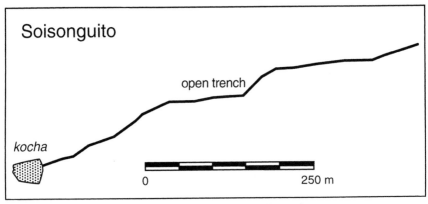

Figure 4.2 Plan of the puquio Soisonguito.

Figure 4.3 Aerial photograph of the puquio Soisonguito taken in March 1970. The single open trench is clearly visible, as is the berm along each flank. The Nasca riverbed lies immediately to the north of the upper end of the puquio. (Photo: Servicio Aerofotográfico Nacional [SAN].)

of an earlier site, dug up in the excavation of the trench, or (2) evidence of small occupations on the berm after puquio construction. In every such case we inspected the exposed stratigraphy of the puquio trench, seeking remains of earlier sites; none were found. The existence of archaeological remains in the case of Soisonguito indicates with little doubt that the berm, and hence the puquio, existed in the Middle Horizon Period and Late Intermediate Period. On the other hand, this does not indicate whether or not the puquio was actually built in the Middle Horizon, or had been in existence for some time prior to that period.

González García noted that filtrations in this portion of the valley were very abundant, citing the high outputs of the puquios Soisongo, Agua Santa, and Ocongalla. Immediately north of Soisonguito he noted the existence of a pond (*charca*), excavated down to the level of the phreatic layer, and also the fact that a small stream emerged on the surface of the riverbed only 1,550 meters from the puquio (González García 1934: 211). Its flow was only 5 liters per second, and he noted that it would have dried up by September, a month after he observed it.

The name of this puquio may derive from the Quechua *sonqo*, which means heart.

Conventillo

The puquio Conventillo lies 7 kilometers to the west of Nasca, watering lands of the same name, and is the only puquio in this sector that lies north of the Nasca River (figure 4.4). It is an open-trench type puquio, measuring 559 meters long,

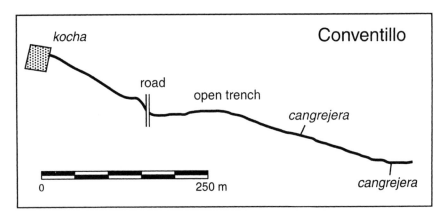

Figure 4.4 Plan of the puquio Conventillo.

and it empties into a large *kocha* (30 x 35 m) that has been reinforced with cement walls. Two small *cangregeras* augment very slightly the quantity of water flowing through this puquio. This puquios capture filtrations located about 6 meters below the surface of the land, about 100 meters north of the riverbed. North of this puquio is a small *pozo-kocha*, nestled up against a natural hill. Visible on the 1944 aerial photographs, it is thus older than other *pozo-kochas* in the region. Local informants knew of no connection between this *pozo-kocha* and the puquio, nor could they tell us when the *pozo-kocha* was excavated.

The lower half of the puquio flows along the southern edge of a large, elongated, sandy mound, probably natural in origin, upon which is located a small modern settlement, also called Conventillo. The puquio provides not only irrigation water but also serves as a source of domestic water for this community. If there was an earlier occupation of this mound, it is no longer visible, being obscured by the modern buildings.

The name of this puquio is Spanish in origin, and it means "small convent."

Agua Santa

The puquio Agua Santa is located to the south of the Nasca River, about 7 kilometers west of Nasca, opposite the puquio Conventillo (figure 4.5). It is an open-trench type puquio, measuring 552 meters long, and it empties into a *kocha*. The phreatic layer is 6 meters deep at this location, and the puquio collects filtrations just 150 meters south of the riverbed. When recorded by González García in 1934, only the lower 240 meters of the puquio were open trench, the rest was filled-trench gallery; he commented, however, that the *ojos* were in a bad state of preservation. The gallery measured 80 cm high and 50 cm wide at that time. Apparently, in the years intervening between his study and the present, the fill over the gallery

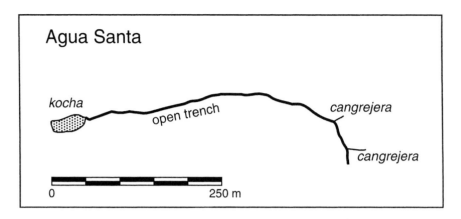

Figure 4.5 Plan of the puquio Agua Santa.

was removed, and the puquio left as an open trench for its entire length. In 1972, under the direction of the Ministry of Agriculture, there were discovered two small galleries (*cangregeras*), lined with huarango wood, entering the puquio from the side, augmenting the volume of water. At present these galleries are exposed as short open trenches.

There are numerous Late Intermediate Period and colonial sherds on the berm near the upper end of this puquio. These are evidence of small occupations and indicate that this puquio was built no later than the Late Intermediate Period.

The output of this puquio is relatively high, and local informants indicate that it was named Agua Santa ("holy water") because it never dries up, even in the worst droughts. According to González García, it produced more water than was needed by its users, so they sold the remainder to Soisongo (1934: 211).

Ocongalla

The puquio Ocongalla is located just south of the Nasca River, about 6 kilometers east of Nasca (figures 4.6 and 4.7). In 1942 Rossel Castro recorded its name as Akonkalla. It is an open-trench type puquio, measuring 592 meters long, and it empties into a small *kocha*. This is not its original *kocha*; the original *kocha* is somewhat larger and located just beyond the present *kocha* (figure 4.7). At its uppermost end, where it penetrates the phreatic layer, the base of the trench lies 6.3 meters below the ground surface, while the filtrations actually occur at a depth of 5.5 meters. As a result, the upper end of the puquio forms a small pond that fills to a depth of about 50 cm before the water flows down the open trench to the *kocha*. The water filters into the puquio through three small *cangrejeras*. (While some local residents, and the occasional engineer, believe that these give evidence of the presence of three galleries that are no longer visible, this is not likely. Local

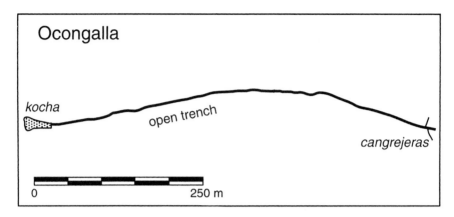

Figure 4.6 Plan of the puquio Ocongalla.

Figure 4.7 Aerial photograph of the puquio Ocongalla, taken in March 1970. The puquio is a single open trench, following along the southern edge of the dry Nasca riverbed. It has a small, subrectangular *kocha* at present, but the irregular field just to the southwest was the original *kocha*. (Photo: SAN.)

users have dug into the trench walls seeking these lost galleries, but they have never found any trace of them.) The abundant filtrations at this location are likely due to the fact that the upper end of the puquio lies immediately adjacent to the riverbed, and it is tapping the underground flow of the Nasca River.

The puquio Ocongalla is an especially charming locale. When one enters the upper trench, the water cascades down the sides of the trench into the small pond, the sounds of running water evoking images of a cool fountain. The large molle trees (*Schinus molle*) growing in and around the puquio provide ample shade and a cool retreat from the heat and wind of the open fields and pampa.

The output of the puquio is relatively high, and it rarely dries up. In the worst of droughts, when the phreatic layer drops slightly in depth and volume, water still filters into the upper portion of the puquio; although it may not flow to the *kocha*, it can be drawn by hand from the pond and provide some water, at least for domestic purposes.

Soisongo: A Converted Puquio

Soisongo is the name of an expanse of arable land in the lower Nasca Valley, lying north of the riverbed, 10 kilometers west of Nasca. The puquio that watered this land in the past no longer functions as a puquio; it has been converted into a *pozo-kocha* by filling in its lower portion and using pumps to extract the water from the upper portion. The phreatic layer lies only 3.82 meters below the surface of the land at this location, according to González García's measurements. As he described it (1934: 210-211) the puquio was an open trench 140 meters long, located just along the south margin of the riverbed, ending at a small *kocha*. In contrast, Rossel Castro describes the puquio "Llapana" (or Yapana, which he probably confused with Soisongo, as we discuss below) as having crossed the riverbed in a subterranean fashion (Rossel Castro 1977: 169) from south to north.

The 1944 air photos offer support for both descriptions: There is visible a possible *kocha*, exactly where González García said it was located. However, if this is so, his published measurement of a length of 140 meters for this puquio must be in error; an estimate of its original length, based on the air photos, is 450 meters. (Perhaps his published measurement was intended to be 440 meters, not 140.) Nevertheless, a *kocha* in this location would be in a position to provide irrigation water for only a very small tract of land; the larger expanse of arable land, that which is called Soisongo, lies on the north side of the riverbed.

Also visible on the 1944 air photos is a stream of water crossing the riverbed from the middle section of the puquio Soisongo, and entering the system of irrigation canals (*acequias*) providing irrigation water to fields north of the river. This may be the actual lower extension of the puquio, providing water to Soisongo, flowing across the surface of the riverbed (in contrast to Rossel Castro's statement that it was subterranean). Regardless, given the fact that puquios usually carry the name of the land they water, it is not unlikely that this puquio indeed watered the tract of land called Soisongo, and it had to cross the bed of the Nasca River in order to do so.

Assuming that the puquio did cross the riverbed, it is understandable that the puquio was not maintained in its original form, once pump technology became available. The section of the puquio that crossed the riverbed must have been destroyed each time the river flowed, entailing great labor costs to rebuild it periodically. Today only the uppermost 178 meters of the puquio remain, the upper portion of which captures the abundant filtrations found in this zone. The puquio is flanked by large berms, larger on the north than the south, the result of the soil extracted during the original construction, and augmented by sediment cleaned periodically out of the puquio. Yet even as we write, this puquio is even less important than in the past: on the north side of the valley, at the highest point in the lands of Soisongo, a very large cement reservoir has been built. It is filled with water pumped directly out of the ground. Thus, Soisongo relies very little on its original puquio.

In the immediate vicinity of the puquio Soisongo, which lies on the lands of the *fundo* Soisonguito, are at least three other *pozo-kochas* (one of which existed in 1944). As we have noted elsewhere, *pozo-kochas* are most prevalent near the upper and lower extremes of the distribution of puquios, generally where the phreatic layer lies closer to the surface.

As in the case of Soisonguito, the name of this puquio may derive from the Quechua *sonqo*, meaning heart. The puquio is also referred to by the name San Antonio.

Ayapana: A Lost Puquio?

If there were additional puquios in the Nasca Irrigation Sector, we would expect to find them farther downstream in the region called Ayapana, located between the current puquios and the reemergence of the river on the surface at Las Cañas. And as the phreatic layer becomes progressively shallower, we also expect to find more construction of *pozo-kochas,* and thus a higher probability of former puquios having been destroyed to make way for the new technology. As pozo-kochas take up much less valuable arable land than puquios, puquios are more likely to have been destroyed where *pozo-kochas* are practicable.

Was there a puquio at Ayapana? The only source that discusses such a puquio is Rossel Castro. In 1942 he called "Yapana" a type of disappeared puquio, and said that there were visible traces of *ojos,* indisputable evidence of a puquio in its "virgin state." In 1977, in contrast, he described the puquio "Llapana" as functioning. In the latter case we suggest that he may have been confusing this Llapana puquio with that which is called Soisongo; his 1977 description conforms with what is visible on aerial photographs of that puquio.

On the other hand, Ayapana comprises a portion of the lower Nasca Valley that is devoid of usable surface water. If this area were under cultivation in the past, then a puquio must have existed there to provide water for irrigation. The aerial photos are inconclusive on this account. In 1944 there is visible what may be an open trench on the south side of the river bank that angles from southeast to northwest toward the riverbed, flows immediately along the south edge of the riverbed for a distance, and then disappears. If the arable land, all of which lies north of the riverbed, were under cultivation, then the puquio water must have been diverted across the dry riverbed to the other side. Traces of this possible puquio are also visible on the 1970 photos. Unfortunately, at present, the location of this possible puquio has been completely modified by the construction of a very large *pozo-kocha,* oriented north-south exactly at the zone of filtration of the possible puquio. No remains are left, if this puquio ever did exist.

We believe it very possible a puquio did exist here, given the presence of both prehistoric and modern settlements adjacent to the arable land of Ayapana, however, we cannot demonstrate this conclusively at this time.

CHAPTER 5

PUQUIOS OF THE AJA IRRIGATION SECTOR

The Aja Irrigation Sector includes all the land from the confluence of the Aja and Tierras Blancas rivers, north of the Tierras Blancas River, upstream to Orcona (figure 5.1). There are sixteen puquios in this sector, plus at least one possible lost puquio. The puquios can be further divided into three groups based on location and productivity. Near the confluence of the rivers are four puquios—Llicuas Norte, Llicuas Sur, San Marcelo, and La Joya de Achaco—that are characterized by especially low output. This is due in part to their location, but more so to the fact that most of them are poorly maintained.

The second group includes the eight puquios in the vicinity of the modern town of Nasca: Achaco, Anglia, Curve, Cuncumayo, Aja, Aja Alto, Bisambra, and Huachuca. The phreatic layer is deeper in this portion of the valley, so some of these puquios, especially Bisambra, are exceptionally long. This portion of the Nasca Valley also, together with the Tierras Blancas Irrigation Sector, includes the widest expanse of arable land along the entire length of the valley. While Cuncumayo and Aja Alto are relatively small and have the lowest output of all the puquios in the Nasca Valley, Anglia and Achaco are very productive, and Bisambra and Aja have the highest output of all of the puquios. It is probably no accident that the Spanish chose to locate their settlement on the tract of land watered by the puquio Bisambra, and adjacent to Aja, in the midst of the most abundant agricultural land in the valley. (The prehispanic inhabitants of the region, on the other hand, chose to locate their settlements on the valley flanks, above the arable valley floor, and in so doing did not reduce the amount of land available for farming.)

The third group is found farther upstream in the Aja Valley, separated from the others by the Quebrada Belén. There are four puquios in this area: Tejeje, Cortez, Vijuna, and Orcona. The first three are located immediately adjacent to a small watercourse called the *riachuelo*, some extending under its bed. This is a distributary of the Aja River that directs water from it toward the Tierras Blancas River; it

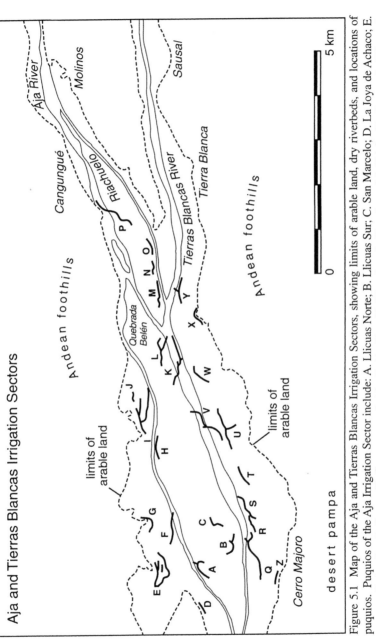

Aja and Tierras Blancas Irrigation Sectors

Figure 5.1 Map of the Aja and Tierras Blancas Irrigation Sectors, showing limits of arable land, dry riverbeds, and locations of puquios. Puquios of the Aja Irrigation Sector include: A. Llicuas Norte; B. Llicuas Sur; C. San Marcelo; D. La Joya de Achaco; E. Achaco; F. Anglia; G. Curve; H. Cuncumayo; I. Aja; J. Aja Alto; K. Bisambra; L. Huachuca; M. Tejeje; N. Cortez; O. Vijuna; P. Orcona. Puquios of the Tierras Blancas Irrigation Sector include: Q. Majoro; R. Majorito; S. Huayrona; T. San Antonio; U. Pangaraví; V. Kallanal; W. La Gobernadora; X. Santo Cristo; Y. Cantalloq. There may have been a puquio at Z. Mojadal.

flows along the north flank of the impervious ridge, La Puntilla, that separates the two drainages. According to González García, filtrations are abundant in the vicinity of the *riachuelo*, which we attribute to the effect of the La Puntilla ridge providing a subsurface barrier and concentrating the subsurface waters at this point. The *riachuelo* shows evidence of having been modified through human activity: in some stretches its course is very straight and of consistent width, suggesting that it was channelized at some time in the past.

The Quebrada Belén is a second distributary that connects the Aja and Tierras Blancas rivers, allowing the higher volume of the Aja River to augment that of the Tierras Blancas River. The waters of at least one puquio (Tejeje) extend across the quebrada to water land on the other side, near the puquio Huachuca. The majority of the water in the Aja River joins the Tierras Blancas via the Quebrada Belén, and one of the areas richest in subsurface filtrations is found near the confluence of the quebrada with the Tierras Blancas River. These filtrations are tapped by two branches of Huachuca, three branches of Bisambra, and possibly two branches of La Gobernadora.

The phreatic layer is shallower in the higher portion of the valley, so the puquios of the third group are therefore shorter than elsewhere. (While Orcona would seem to be an exception, we will demonstrate that its total length is misleading.) In the past few years several *pozo-kochas* have been excavated in this sector, tapping the relatively shallow phreatic layer. There is some concern on the part of the users of the puquios that these will cause the water level to drop in depth and render the puquios unusable. This has not happened, however, and puquios in this upper zone maintain good to very good output. There are reports of one, and possibly two, lost puquios just upstream from the currently functioning puquios.

Llicuas Norte

The puquio Llicuas Norte is located south of the Aja River, just east of its confluence with the Tierras Blancas River, 3.5 kilometers west of Nasca (figure 5.2). This is Gonzalez García's Llicuas #1, and it is also called Pikiman. Emptying into a small elongated *kocha* is an open trench, 349 meters long. Above the open trench, the puquio is a subterranean gallery that was apparently constructed first as an open trench, then refilled; it measures 128 meters long, and has 16 or 17 *ojos* at present. (Due to dense vegetation on the surface, not all *ojos* were easily visible at the time our study was made.) At this point two branches flow together. The longer southern branch is at least 131 meters long, is of filled-trench type construction, and has at least four *ojos*. (The density of vegetation on the surface prevented us from being able to determine its exact length and number of *ojos*.) The northern branch entering from the north measures 127 meters and has 4 *ojos;* it is of tunneled construction, and may actually extend under the bed of the Aja River.

This puquio, like the others in this sector, has relatively low output. This may

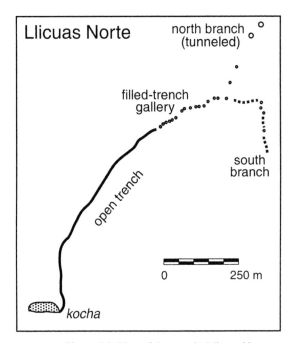

Figure 5.2 Plan of the puquio Llicuas Norte.

be due to its location with regard to the subsurface hydrological regime, as in this portion of the valley filtrations seem to be more abundant to the south of the Tierras Blancas River than to the north near the Aja River. However, the low productivity of this puquio may be equally well due to the fact that it is so poorly maintained. Interestingly, it was also poorly maintained in 1934 when González García made his observations of it.

Llicuas Sur

The puquio Llicuas Sur is located between the Aja and Tierras Blancas rivers, just east of their confluence, 3.5 kilometers west-southwest of Nasca (figure 5.3). Emptying into a small *kocha* is an open trench, 272 meters long. Above the open trench is a filled-trench gallery that extends for 27 meters to the first *ojo*, at which point two branches flow together. The branch that enters from the north is only 43 meters long, with a single *ojo*. The longer southern branch measures 173 meters long with 7 *ojos*. Some of the *ojos* have been reconstructed with cement tubes, and are no longer in their original condition. However, inspection of the 1944 aerial photographs indicates quite clearly that Llicuas Sur was originally built as an open trench.

Like the other three puquios in this sector, Llicuas Sur has relatively low out-

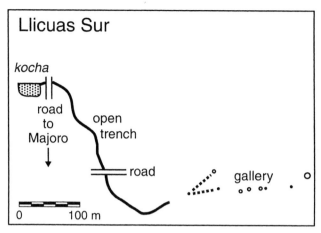

Figure 5.3 Plan of the puquio Llicuas Sur.

put. However, at the time we observed it, it was apparent that the gallery had not been cleaned in some years, which could account for reduced output.

San Marcelo

The puquio San Marcelo is located between the Aja and Tierras Blancas rivers, some 3 kilometers west-southwest of Nasca (figure 5.4). It has no *kocha,* so our measurements begin where the puquio trench opens into the acequias that water the adjacent fields. The open trench measures 337 meters long, and the gallery, which is of filled-trench type construction, measures 96 meters long. Due to the density of overgrowth on the surface, it was not possible to count the number of *ojos* in the gallery portion of the puquio, and its total length is probably greater than we were able to measure. While González García measured this puquio as being 790 meters long, the lack of a *kocha,* and hence the lack of a clear terminus, accounts for the differences between his measurements and ours. About halfway along the current puquio is a small dam creating a pool from which water is pumped to the surface.

La Joya de Achaco

The puquio La Joya de Achaco is located north of the Aja River, opposite the puquio Llicuas Norte, about 4 kilometers west of Nasca. It is an open-trench type puquio, some 260 meters long, with a small *kocha* (figure 5.5). It was not recorded as a puquio by González García, or any of the researchers that came after him. In fact, we first regarded it as being only a *sangradera*—a trench used for "bleeding" excess irrigation water off agricultural fields—and modern, at that.

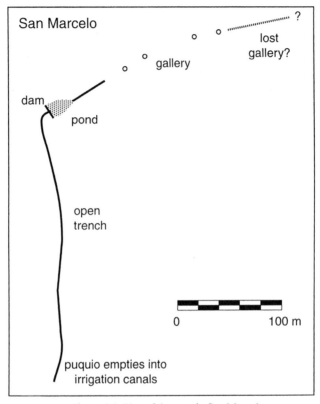

Figure 5.4 Plan of the puquio San Marcelo.

However, while it does serve as a *sangradera*, it is apparently a puquio as well, given that it does intersect the phreatic layer and is provided with filtrations from it. It is, however, much shorter and shallower than all other puquios, and can function only in especially wet years when the phreatic layer is higher. When we recorded the puquio in 1993 we were told that the output of this puquio was the lowest of all the puquios and that it had been dry for several decades. We were also told that it has a gallery segment, but we observed no evidence of this.

Perhaps at the time of the earlier studies this puquio was dried up and not in use, or it was so insignificant that González García chose not to devote any effort to it. But it is especially significant that because González García did not record this puquio, or the puquio today called Santo Cristo, many later investigators do not mention them either. This helps us to identify which researchers were merely following the work of González García and which investigators conducted their own field investigations. Moreover, even today its output is not regularly measured by the Junta de Usarios, the local agency charged with recording puquio output every month.

Figure 5.5 Oblique aerial photograph of the puquio La Joya de Achaco.

Achaco

The puquio Achaco is located north of the Aja River, 3.5 kilometers west-north-west of Nasca (figures 5.6 and 5.7; see also figure 3.2). Topographically it lies adjacent to an impervious ridge that extends into the valley, which may serve to direct subsurface water to this point, resulting in abundant filtrations. Entering the

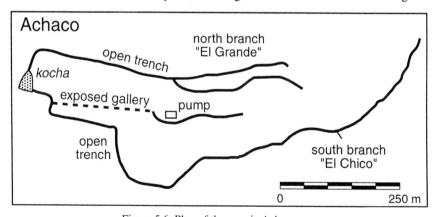

Figure 5.6 Plan of the puquio Achaco.

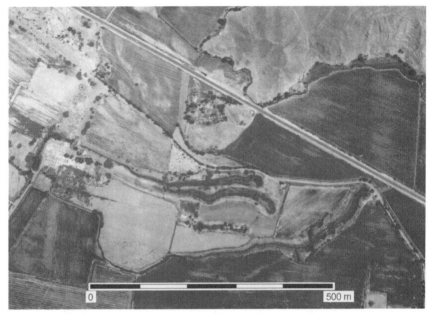

Figure 5.7 Aerial photograph of Achaco taken in March 1970. Two large trenches join to form the northern puquio, called El Grande. The southern puquio is a very long trench that begins adjacent to the Pan American Highway; it is called "El Chico" due to its lower volume of water. Between the two is another trench that currently serves as a *pozo-kocha;* there are traces of a gallery that once connected it with the same *kocha* shared by the others. On the hillsides to the northeast are located settlements dating to the Late Intermediate Period. (Photo: SAN.)

large *kocha* are two open trenches, one from the north, the other from the south, called El Grande and El Chico, respectively; these names refer to the relative volume of water carried in each, not to their relative length. The northern trench is 354 meters long, to the confluence of two parallel open trenches: the one entering from the left measures 223 meters long and the one from the right measures 294 meters long. The trench, El Chico, that enters the *kocha* from the south is 1,025 meters long, with one small *cangregera.*

Between the two main branches is a short *pozo-kocha* from which water is pumped; apparently it was so at the time of González García's study, making it the first clearly identified *pozo-kocha* in the valley. He was told that it was the remains of a lost puquio, but disregarded this possibility (González García 1934: 213). In recent years, however, remains of a gallery connecting the *pozo-kocha* to the lower end of El Chico have been uncovered, suggesting that it may once have formed a separate branch of the puquio. Additionally, there are traces visible on 1944 aerial photos of what appears to have been another trench to the south of El Chico, and joining with it.

The output of Achaco, especially from the northern branches, is not only relatively high but also apparently quite reliable. González García (1934: 213-214) reported that during the terrible drought of 1860-1864 all the puquios except Achaco dried up.

Along the upper portion of the northernmost branch is a large berm, formed from the soil excavated from the original trench, and augmented by sediment removed during periodic cleaning of the puquio. Eroding out of the berm are numerous artifacts pertaining to the Late Intermediate Period, indicating that a small settlement may have been located on the berm at that time. As in the case of other puquios, this is evidence for prehispanic use of the puquios, but future excavation may enable us to clarify the nature and extent of such occupations.

Anglia

The puquio Anglia lies just north of the Aja River, 2.5 kilometers west of Nasca (figures 5.8 and 5.9). It is a trench and gallery type puquio that flows from east to west, with two short side branches. Its *kocha* is large and lined with cement; it is said that for a number of years a penguin made this *kocha* its home. Entering the *kocha* from the east is an open trench that measures 479 meters to the point where a *cangregera*, 20 meters long, enters from the left. The main trench continues another 76 meters where it becomes a filled-trench type gallery for 36 meters, with three visible *ojos;* a second *cangregera*, 27 meters long, enters this stretch from the north (figure 5.10). In several areas the fill over the gallery has been removed and short stretches of open trench have been exposed. The last 4.3 meters of visible puquio are of tunneled construction, ending at a single *ojo.* This *ojo* is not the actual beginning of the puquio because the water in it is clearly flowing from a point farther to the east. Several informants told us that the gallery continues at least 100 meters farther, penetrating under the riverbed of the Aja River, and extending to the point where the modern Pan-American Highway bridge crosses the river. Indeed, Rossel Castro was told the same thing (1942: 198; 1977: 183). The fact that this puquio is of relatively high productivity is consistent with the penetration of its gallery beneath the riverbed, where filtrations should be especially abundant.

There are small numbers of Middle Horizon Period and Late Intermediate

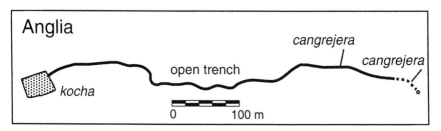

Figure 5.8 Plan of the puquio Anglia.

Figure 5.9 Aerial photograph of the puquios Anglia and Curve taken in March
1970. Curve begins along the east side of the bedrock outcropping extending into
the valley from the north; it curves around to the west and flows to a *kocha;* a
small modern settlement is located just south of the *kocha.* The puquio Anglia is
visible as a single open trench ending at a *kocha,* also with an associated settlement; the upper end of the puquio is said to begin under the riverbed near the
bridge. The linear feature crossing the photo between the puquios is the Pan
American Highway. Sites dating to the Late Intermediate Period are located on
the hill flanks to the north. (Photo: SAN.)

Period artifacts along the north berm, indicating small ephemeral occupations on
the raised berm during those periods.

Figure 5.10 Cangrejera of the puquio Anglia entering from the north. Archaeologist Dr. Mary Van Buren is seen at the end of the branch.

Curve

The puquio Curve (called Kurpe by Rossel Castro in 1942) is located north of the Aja River, 2.5 kilometers northwest of Nasca, adjacent to an impervious promontory that extends perpendicularly into the Nasca Valley (figures 5.11 and 5.12; see also figure 5.9). The puquio is an open trench its entire length of 541 meters. It begins along the east flank of the promontory, flowing first south and then west around the end of the promontory, and northwest to the *kocha*. The trench is deeper than usual, measuring more than 10 meters deep (figure 5.13). There are abundant filtrations, and the water filters into the puquio with some pressure, like an artesian spring. To demonstrate this, one informant tossed a softball-sized rock into the trench, and water bubbled up at the point of its impact. González García noted that the water filtered into the puquio at a depth of only 2.2 meters below the surface of the land (1934: 214), quite a bit higher than our observation. In recent years the *kocha* has been enlarged and reinforced with cement. Access to the puquio was enhanced by the 1986 CORDEICA project, and it is now visited by tourists.

There is a large Late Intermediate Period village located on the hills flanking the valley north of the *kocha* of this puquio, and a small site of that period adjacent to the upper end of the puquio.

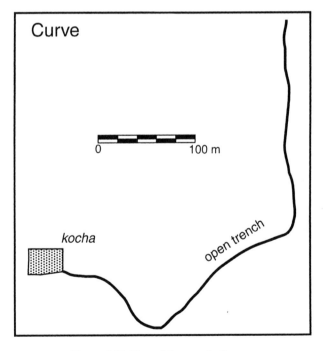

Figure 5.11 Plan of the puquio Curve.

Figure 5.12 Oblique aerial photograph of the puquio Curve.

Figure 5.13 The upper end of the trench of the puquio Curve. The pickup truck
parked on the surface gives an indication of the scale and depth of the puquio.

Cuncumayo

The puquio Cuncumayo (sometimes called San Mauricio) is located just south of the Aja River, 1 kilometer northwest of the Plaza de Armas of Nasca, and it lies within the northern outskirts of the town (figure 5.14). It is a trench type puquio, measuring 537 meters long. At the time of our study there was water to be found only in the upper portion of the puquio; the rest of the puquio was dry, as was the *kocha*. It appears that the *kocha* has not been used in some years, and that the water, when it is available, flows directly into the system of *acequias*. The output

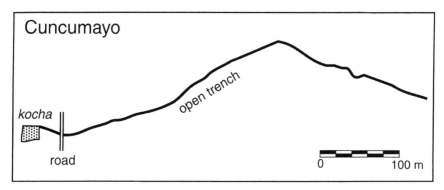

Figure 5.14 Plan of the puquio Cuncumayo.

of this puquio is quite low at present; given its location adjacent to the Aja River, we would expect its output to be much higher. However, it is also the case that the puquio has not been well maintained, and its flow might be improved substantially were it cleaned more regularly.

According to González García (1934: 214), in 1906 a tenant of the Cuncumayo *fundo* suspected that there was originally a gallery section above the known puquio, and he undertook excavations on the hacienda Bisambra, through whose lands the puquio flowed, to find it. According to the story told to González García, he was successful. However, the owner of that hacienda was opposed to these excavations, filed suit, and the tenant was obliged to fill them back in. If it is true that this puquio was once longer than it is at present, but that the gallery section has fallen into disuse, this could explain the low output of this puquio. However we see no evidence of its having a lost gallery, nor has one been reported to us.

Aja

The puquio Aja (written "Aka" by Rossel Castro in 1942) is located immediately north of the Aja River, just over 1 kilometer northwest of the Plaza de Armas of

Nasca (figure 5.15). It is a trench and gallery type puquio, presently of three branches, that flows into a *kocha*. Since this puquio has been modified in recent years, we shall describe it first as it was before the modification. At the time of the study of González García, and as visible on aerial photographs from 1944, this puquio might well be considered two separate puquios that shared the same name and the same *kocha;* we will refer to these as Aja Norte and Aja Sur. The northern puquio is a trench type puquio with two branches. From the *kocha* upstream, the open trench measures 488 meters, at which point two parallel branches join together. The branch entering from the left (north) measures 83 meters in length, that from the right (south) 170 meters. The southern puquio originally entered the *kocha* from the south, and it was a trench and gallery type puquio whose length was given by González García as 577 meters. (In point of fact, we estimate its length at the time of González García's study to have been on the order of 750 meters of open trench, and 266 meters of gallery.) There is no plan or vertical cut of this puquio in González García's published report; but one, probably drawn by González García, is published by Rossel Castro (1977: 182).

Sometime between 1944 and 1970, Aja Sur was rerouted. It no longer flows directly to the *kocha,* but it is diverted abruptly northward to flow into Aja Norte about 500 meters east of the *kocha.* Its present length is 509 meters of open trench, from its confluence with the northern branch to the gallery. Then it continues as tunneled gallery for 266 meters, with 17 *ojos.* It is not unlikely that this branch actually begins beneath the bed of the Aja River, as local informants claim, and as Rossel Castro wrote (1977: 182). Rossel Castro described the interior of the gallery as measuring 70 cm high and 60 cm wide.

The low output measurement (10 liters per second) of González García deserves some comment. According to his report, he measured the flow of water at a point 50 meters upstream from the *kocha,* but we do not know which of the two puquios he was measuring. Current measurements (70 liters per second), which

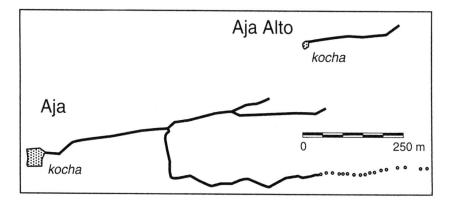

Figure 5.15 Plan of the puquios Aja and Aja Alto.

represent the combined total of the flow of both puquios, would make it seem that this is one of the most productive puquios in the region. We have observed that the greater quantity of water emanates from Aja Sur, but separate measurements of flow from the two puquios are not available. González García (1934: 215) stated that the southern branch was usually dry from October until December, but modern informants differ, saying that this branch is very productive and rarely dries up. We suspect that at the time of his study the southern branch was not well maintained, and his data were affected accordingly, or that he was measuring the northern puquio.

The name of this puquio, Aja, is probably a Quechua variant of the Spanish word, *agua* (water).

Aja Alto

The puquio Aja Alto (also called Carrizal) is located north of the Aja River, and just northeast of the puquio Aja, 1.25 kilometers northwest of the Plaza de Armas of Nasca (see figure 5.15). It is an open-trench type puquio, only 246 meters long, that flows into a small *kocha*. It has the lowest output of any puquio, except perhaps La Joya de Achaco. Its present owner says that in recent years its output has decreased even further, caused, he says, by the excavation of a well a few hundred meters to the southeast.

A short distance to the northwest are a group of low hills, around which the ground is always moist. Perhaps if the puquio had been built a little closer to those hills its productivity might have been higher.

Bisambra

The puquio Bisambra (spelled Wisampra by Rossel Castro in 1942) is located along and under the Tierras Blancas River, and its *kocha* lies only about 1/2 kilometer east of the Plaza de Armas of Nasca (figure 5.16). It is a gallery type puquio, one of the longest in the region, and, with Aja, one of the two most productive. The 1986 CORDEICA accomplished a more extensive cleaning of this puquio than had been undertaken in many years, and a map was made of the portions of the puquio that were cleaned (Solar 1997: 242). Because most of this puquio is not visible on the surface, we were able to record in detail only the lowermost portion of the puquio.

The *kocha* of the puquio is large and reinforced with cement walls. In about 1994 the height of the retaining walls was raised to increase the capacity of the *kocha,* but in doing so the lower portion of the open trench has become submerged

The open trench enters the *kocha* from the east, flowing into the southeast corner of the *kocha.* The open trench extends to the east and then bends south, for

Figure 5.16 Aerial photograph of the puquio Bisambra taken in March 1970. Visible and mapped portions of the puquio are indicated, as are the locations of two possible lost branches. (Photo: SAN.)

a total distance of 209 meters, at which point it becomes a filled-trench gallery. Nearly all of the open trench lies behind tall adobe walls on private property, so it is difficult to see at present. The recent construction of the Italian Archaeological Research Center over the uppermost section of open trench has restricted the access of local residents to this portion of the puquio, traditionally used as a place to launder clothes. While an area was left open expressly for this purpose, the local residents have expressed some displeasure over the decrease in their access to the puquio.

The gallery portion of the puquio continues to the south and then bends east, paralleling the riverbed, to the north of the modern levee that forms the riverbank. However, before the riverbed was narrowed through the construction of the artificial levees, the puquio flowed along the northern edge of the riverbed. The construction of levees has reclaimed the land along the river's edge, and today the trajectory of the puquio is covered with modern houses. The residents of the houses use the *ojos* of the puquio as wells from which to draw water for domestic use. Unfortunately, the *ojos* are also used for the disposal of waste, thus contaminating the waters of the puquio. There are presently eight *ojos* along this 210 meter long stretch of the puquio, which is of filled-trench construction.

There are no *ojos* along the next 100 meters of the gallery, as the puquio angles toward the present riverbed, passing under the modern levees. A single *ojo* was found and opened by CORDEICA, near the present northern bank of the riverbed. At this point the gallery turns southward and crosses to the modern levee marking the present south bank of the riverbed. Within this 40 meter long stretch a branch enters from the north.

This northern branch was reported to González García (1934: 220) by an old man named Vicente Suárez Cervantes, who was eighty-four years old at the time of González García's study. This man said that when he was young he held the office of "pasador," a member of the team that cleaned the puquio. He entered the gallery of Bisambra and crawled through a distance he estimated to be about 200 meters. At that point two branches joined. The one from the right, from Cantalloq, was nearly full of mud. The one from the left he was able to enter and follow some unknown distance; he said it was directed toward Belén. The remains of berms still visible on the surface near the puquio Huachuca (see figure 5.18, below) indicate both the location of this now-abandoned branch, and the fact that it was originally of open trench construction.

Beneath the southern river levee the main gallery angles to the southeast for about 50 meters, at which point it turns eastward, and a second branch enters from the south. This branch is no longer in use, but there are remains of berms extending to the southeast and bending to the east for a total distance of some 600 meters, allowing us to trace the trajectory of this branch, which was originally of open trench construction.

The main gallery—the only branch still functioning at present—extends eastward and passes under reclaimed land, now covered with modern houses. Originally the puquio followed the southern edge of the Tierras Blancas riverbed. The ultimate end of the puquio is unknown, and lies somewhere in the vicinity of Cantalloq, but the CORDEICA project cleaned and mapped only an additional 510 meters of the gallery. There are nine *ojos* in this last stretch of the puquio, but all have been lined with cement tubes, and they appear more like wells than *ojos* on the surface. This long branch of Bisambra may have been of tunneled construction, but modern improvements have obscured the evidence that would allow us to say this with absolute certainty.

It is worth noting at this point that the artificial levees were constructed sometime between 1944 and 1970. The effect of these levees has been to reduce the width of the riverbed more than 75 percent (see figure 5.18, below). While the riverbed is usually dry, this does not normally present a problem. However, when the river does flood, the reduced width of the bed forces the flow to increase in depth and velocity, with the result that once the water races past the town of Nasca, protected by the levees, it explodes out from this chute, devastating the defenseless terrain below.

The location of this puquio is puzzling. The Tierras Blancas riverbed was very wide before construction of the levees, and the puquio flowed under it, along the northern edge, thence to the other side, and continued under the riverbed the along its southern edge. If this puquio was originally built as an open trench, then it would have been inundated every time the river flowed, if the riverbed was the same width in earlier times. Here we raise the possibility that perhaps the riverbed was much narrower in ancient times, and that during the terrible El Niño flooding of the 1300's AD (Satterlee et al. 2001) the Aja River jumped its banks, creating the Quebrada Belén, joining with the Tierras Blancas River, and scouring out a much wider bed. If this were the case, then the puquio may have sat above, rather than in, the riverbed prior to this time, except for the point of crossing. Alternatively, if the riverbed were very wide at the time of construction of the long branch of the puquio, then the puquio must have been a covered gallery for most of its length.

The output of Bisambra was the highest of any measured by González García, and it ranks among the highest in current output records. Its waters irrigate all the land between the two rivers, reaching all the way to San Marcelo. Because of the continued growth of the town of Nasca, injudiciously placed by the Spanish on some of the most valuable agricultural land in the valley, progressively less land is under cultivation. As a result, there is water available from the puquio Bisambra for a more extended range of land. While domestic water for the settlement of Nasca was originally provided by Bisambra, potable water is now drawn from deep wells, and the puquio water is used primarily for agricultural purposes.

The puquio Bisambra holds an important place in local beliefs about water, and its water is said to be sacred. It is believed that drinking the waters of Bisambra will cause a person to become enamored of Nasca, and, should they ever chance to leave Nasca, they will always return. It is not uncommon at social gatherings in Nasca to observe small plastic bags of water from Bisambra suspended from the rafters.

The name Bisambra is said by some to mean "gravelly terrain."

Huachuca

The puquio Huachuca is located just north of the Tierras Blancas River, 1.25 kilometers east-northeast of Nasca (figures 5.17 and 5.18). It is a trench and gallery type puquio with two main branches, one flowing north and then west, and the other flowing northwest. The *kocha* of Huachuca is, at this writing, one of the few *kochas* that remains in an unimproved state; that is, it is not reinforced with cement walls. The open trench enters the *kocha* from the east, and is 294 meters long to the point where the two branches join. The northern branch, entering from the left, extends another 265 meters as open trench, then angles sharply toward the river and becomes filled-trench gallery, with only 6 *ojos,* for another 173 meters.

The southern branch also continues as open trench, for 48 meters, then it becomes a filled-trench gallery for 299 meters more, with 23 *ojos.* Remains of a

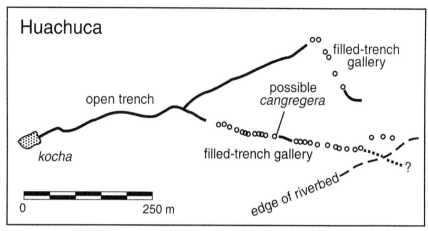

Figure 5.17 Plan of the puquio Huachuca.

Figure 5.18 Aerial photograph of the puquio Huachuca taken in March 1970. The *kocha* is visible in the upper left corner. The puquio comprises two main branches; the southern branch is actually formed by one branch visible on the surface, and a second that extends under the riverbed with no surface traces. Note the canalization of the riverbed. The lighter colored mounds to the southeast of the *kocha* probably mark the location of the lost north branch of Bisambra. (Photo: SAN.)

berm on the surface suggest that a short *cangregera* entered from the left (north) about halfway along this stretch. At this point a small branch, 83 meters long, enters from the left, marked on the surface by three *ojos*. The main branch continues on its southeasterly trajectory to, and perhaps under, the bed of the Tierras Blancas River, at least another 150 meters, according to informants. Its ultimate end is unknown, in part because of damage caused by the flooding river. Rossel Castro reported that the interior of the gallery measured 70 cm high and 60 cm wide (1942: 197). González García's diagram of this puquio indicates that it was 8.55 meters deep along the north branch, some 150 meters from its end (1934: Plano 4). At the time of González García's study, only the first 312 meters of the puquio above the *kocha* were open trench—the remainder was gallery. This is an instance in which we can see that modern modifications have included removing the fill from filled-trench segments of gallery, leaving exposed the open trench. González García (1934: 215) also reported that just three years before his study a worker, named Palomino, cleaning the puquio had been killed in a cave-in in the gallery. It took three days, and great expense, to recover the body.

The output of this puquio is relatively high, but not nearly as high as the puquios of Bisambra or Aja. At the time of González García's study it ranked as the fifth highest in terms of output, but today it ranks in the lower half of puquios in the Nasca Valley. This may be due in part to lack of maintenance and also to the fact that the urban sprawl of Nasca has encroached on the south branch, and the puquio has become a place of garbage and waste disposal.

Most of the water from this puquio is now diverted across the Tierras Blancas River to water lands to the south, as the town of Nasca has covered much of its original terrain.

The name of this puquio is said to mean "water that flows" or "house of clay."

Tejeje

The puquio Tejeje is located between the *riachuelo* and the Quebrada Belén, 2.5 kilometers east-northeast of Nasca (figure 5.19). (Its name was spelled "Tekeke" by Rossel Castro in 1942, and it is also called by the name, Belén, for the land that it waters.) It is a trench and gallery type puquio, flowing generally east to west. From the *kocha* a major *acequia* carries nearly all of its water across the Quebrada Belén to the former hacienda of the same name. The hacienda buildings sit on a natural mound; while no remains are visible on the surface of this mound, excavation might provide evidence of earlier settlement associated with this puquio.

Entering the *kocha* from the east is an open trench that measures 369 meters in length. Above this point the puquio is a gallery of filled-trench type, extending another 152 meters, with four *ojos*. Its origin lies very near, or perhaps beneath, the *riachuelo*. At the time the puquio was recorded by González García (1934: 215-216) he said that just above the point where the gallery meets the open trench

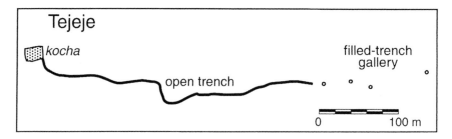

Figure 5.19   Plan of the puquio Tejeje.

a second branch entered from the south, and that this branch passed under the bed of the *riachuelo*. It is also reported that a third branch enters from the north, but we have found no evidence of this.

He also said that this puquio was one of those in the worst condition, and it was desperately in need of cleaning; this was reiterated by Rossel Castro (1942: 197; 1977: 178). González García reported that water was flowing ("bleeding") out of the ground into the *riachuelo,* and this was clearly the result of blockage inside the gallery, forcing the water to back up and seep out. In fact, this is where he took his output measurement, so it is probably not as reliable as those of other puquios. (In contrast to his measurement of 10 liters per second measured in the *riachuelo,* he measured only two liters per second flowing through the open trench of the puquio, just below the point where it became gallery.)

Cortez

The puquio Cortez is located just north of the *riachuelo,* 3.25 kilometers east-northeast of Nasca (figure 5.20). Alternate names include El Cerco (González García), and Uchuya (Rossel Castro 1942). It is a trench and filled-trench gallery type puquio, flowing west, northwest, and west to a *kocha.* It presently has only a single branch that enters the *kocha* as an open trench 244 meters long. Above this point it is a gallery of filled-trench type, with four *ojos,* that measures 57 meters long. When recorded by González García (1934: 216) it was a long open trench with a second branch entering from the south near its upper end. The current puquio comprises only the south branch, with a new *kocha* built near the point where it originally joined the main trench. The main trench and north branch recorded by González García no longer function.

In 1934 González García wrote that the users of this puquio, which was very deficient in output, diverted water from the *riachuelo* into the *kocha* to augment their supply of water (1934: 216). Rossel Castro, based on his observations of 1942, says that there was no *kocha* (1942: 197; 1977: 178). Thus we conclude that the new *kocha* was built sometime after that date.

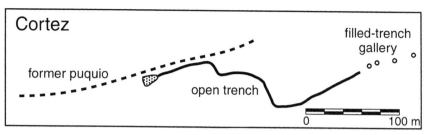

Figure 5.20 Plan of the puquio Cortez.

Vijuna

The puquio Vijuna (called Matara by Rossel Castro in 1942) is located just north of the *riachuelo,* 4 kilometers east-northeast of Nasca (figure 5.21). It is a trench and gallery type puquio, flowing southwest to west. At the time of our study we were most fortunate to have as our informant Señor Carlos Jiménez, who lives adjacent to the puquio, and who has been inside its gallery. The puquio has no *kocha* at present, and the waters flow directly into the system of *acequias.* However, at the time of González García's study it did have a functioning *kocha,* and its remains are clearly visible. The *kocha* was not kept cleaned and gradually filled in with sediment, so for the past forty years or so it has not functioned as a *kocha.* At present it shelters a small kitchen garden, and the puquio becomes an *acequia* flowing through it.

Beginning at the point where the puquio originally entered its *kocha* from the east, the puquio is an open trench 229 meters long, flowing generally from east to west. Along this stretch a short (6 meters long) *cangregera* enters from the south, marked by a single *ojo.* It in turn is formed by two short branches 10 and 15

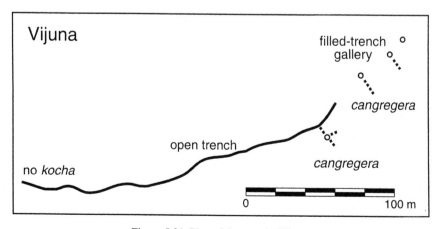

Figure 5.21 Plan of the puquio Vijuna.

meters long, respectively. Informants say that the main puquio trench was originally gallery, but it fell in and so was left open.

Above the open trench portion of the puquio, it continues to the northeast as a
gallery of filled-trench type construction, judging by the large berm of soil that
parallels its course; the gallery measures 60 meters long and has three *ojos*. At the
lowermost *ojo* a *cangregera* enters from the south; it is said to be about 15 meters
long, but there are no visible traces of it on the surface. Likewise, by the second or
third *ojo* another *cangregera* enters, this one about 10 meters in length. Beyond
the third *ojo* the gallery probably continues for perhaps another 100 meters, bending around to the north, following alongside the berm visible on the surface. Only
the first 50 meters or so of this section are cleaned, so its total length is unknown.
According to González García's plan of this puquio, it was 5.77 meters deep at the
uppermost *ojo* open at that time (1934: Plano 5).

The output of this puquio is relatively high, due in part to the fact that it is well
maintained.

Orcona

The puquio Orcona is located beneath and immediately south of the Aja River, 4.5
kilometers east-northeast of Nasca (figures 5.22). It is a trench and gallery type
puquio, flowing generally to the southwest. The phreatic layer is relatively shallow in this region, being at the uppermost end of the distribution of puquios. Orcona
is among the shallowest of the puquios, lying only about 4 meters below the riverbed at its upper end. For much of its course it lies so close to the surface that water
can be diverted out of it at several points before it reaches its *kocha.* Thus its total
length is deceptively long.

The *kocha,* which is called Matara, was dry at the time of our study, all the
puquio water having been diverted out of the open trench at two points along its
course. The now dry open trench enters the *kocha* from the northeast, and measures 278 meters long. At this point the remaining water is diverted out of the
trench and into the system of *acequias.* Above this point the puquio continues as
an open trench for another 299 meters, to another point where water is diverted
into *acequias.* Between these two diversion points the puquio has been rerouted to
skirt the adjacent fields; its original course followed a more direct route.

Extending upstream from the last diversion point, which could be considered the effective end of the puquio—the point at which it intersects the level
of the ground surface—the puquio continues as an open trench for 217 meters.
From this point upward it is a filled-trench type gallery for 70 meters, sections of which have fallen in and been left open as short segments of open
trench. The next section of gallery measures 60 meters with three *ojos* reaching the edge of the riverbed. Rossel Castro reported that the gallery interior was

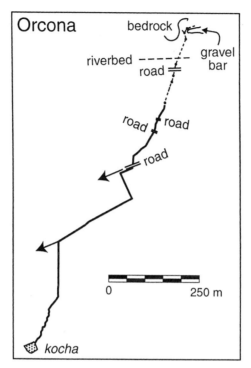

Figure 5.22 Plan of the puquio Orcona.

1 meter high and 40 cm wide.

The gallery continues beneath the riverbed for 86 meters; three *ojos* were opened along this stretch during the CORDEICA cleaning in 1986, allowing the mapping of its trajectory under the riverbed (figure 5.23). At this last point two branches join. The branch from the left, which is only 12 meters long, apparently begins right against the impervious outcropping called Cerro Orcona. (In fact, it is this hill that gives the terrain, and hence the puquio, its name. Its name, derived from the Quechua *urqu*, meaning hill, translates to mean "place of the hill.") We were told that a high volume of water issues from the valley side right at the hill, perhaps evidence of the fault-directed water identified by Johnson et al. (2002).

The branch that enters from the right follows the course of the riverbed, and extends another 13 meters to the last *ojo* opened by CORDEICA. The total length of this branch is about 70 meters, but its construction technique remains unclear. Informants report that its output is lower than that of the other branch.

This puquio was extensively refurbished by CORDEICA for two reasons. First, it had been badly damaged by flooding in the early 1980s. Because this puquio is located farthest upstream, it is more subject to flood damage, bearing the brunt of the first advent of floodwaters flowing down the Aja River. The puquio has no large berm, owing to the fact that it is very shallow, and the excavation of the

Figure 5.23 Oblique aerial photograph of the uppermost portion of the puquio
Orcona showing the open *ojos* in the bed of the Aja River.

trench produced relatively little soil to be piled up to protect the puquio on its
vulnerable flank.

Second, the puquio is accessible from the town, and it was thought that tourists could be induced to include it in their itinerary of sights and sites to be seen in
Nasca. The *ojos* were therefore refurbished in elegant, if not original, stonework,
and provided with steps so that tourists might view the interior of the gallery.
While tourism to Orcona did increase at first, the *ojos* have not been maintained,
and they are often strewn with garbage and waste. Flooding in 1994 has made
access to Orcona very difficult, so few tourists see it at present.

The output of the puquio Orcona is relatively high, and it waters an especially
extensive terrain with a large number of users.

Possible Puquios above Orcona

As discussed earlier, the places we should most expect to find traces of lost or
destroyed puquios are in the uppermost and lowermost portions of their range. In
these areas the phreatic layer is shallow enough that wells and pumps can be used
to extract the water from *pozo-kochas,* without the loss of arable land taken up by
puquio trenches.

About 1 kilometer upstream from Orcona are some mounds of soil that may or may not be the remains of a puquio trench or kocha. According to a reliable informant, the former *mayordomo* of the hacienda Orcona, a section of gallery was located in this area, called Cangungue, some years ago. No further investigation was made, however. We have not seen this gallery ourselves, but we think it reasonable to suppose that it did exist. We must entertain the possibility, however, that this reported gallery is an upper extension of Orcona.

Farther upstream, at Molinos, there is an impervious outcropping that extends in the Aja Valley from its south flank. This is the sort of location where one might expect a puquio, since the outcropping would form a point where water would be concentrated, and therefore reliably found. There are ambiguous traces on the 1944 aerial photograph, so we cannot determine whether or not a puquio once existed at this location. Above this point the valley narrows, and there is no room for puquio construction. Indeed, from this point upward, there is generally sufficient water flowing in the river to support limited agriculture.

CHAPTER 6

PUQUIOS OF THE TIERRAS BLANCAS IRRIGATION SECTOR

The puquios of the Tierras Blancas Irrigation Sector are located south of the Tierras Blancas River, extending from the confluence of the Aja and Tierras Blancas rivers east to Cantalloq, just at the western tip of the ridge La Puntilla (see figure 5.1). There are nine puquios in this sector: Majoro, Majorito, Huayrona, San Antonio, Pangaraví, Kallanal, La Gobernadora, Santo Cristo, and Cantalloq, plus there is one possible lost puquio at Mojadal. These puquios vary widely in output, due in part to differences in maintenance, with reduced output in poorly maintained puquios. But several puquios with relatively high output have branches that extend beneath the riverbed, providing them with more abundant filtrations.

Majoro

The puquio Majoro (also called Majoro Grande) is located just south of the Tierras Blancas River, 4 kilometers southwest of Nasca (figure 6.1). It is a trench and gallery type puquio, flowing generally from east to west, and it has two branches. The *kocha* today is surrounded by the buildings of the former hacienda Majoro, now the Hotel de la Borda. It was lined with cement and painted blue, and it served as the swimming pool of the former hacienda; an artificial island in the *kocha* is connected to the land by an arched wooden bridge. In its current condition, the *kocha* of Majoro is certainly unique among all the puquios. The open trench enters the *kocha* from the east, and it is 907 meters long. Above this point it is a filled-trench gallery, extending another 96 meters, with 7 *ojos,* to the point where the two main branches join.

   The longer, southern branch of the puquio extends generally east, meandering slightly, for 142 meters; it is of filled-trench construction, with nine *ojos.* A tenth *ojo* is located another 104 meters to the east. According to informants the gallery

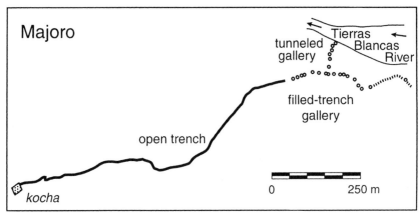

Figure 6.1 Plan of the puquio Majoro.

bends northward then south again in this stretch, so its actual length is probably longer than our straight-line measurement. This last stretch of the gallery may be of tunneled construction. The puquio is said to continue above the last *ojo,* to the southeast toward the open trench of Majorito, but its ultimate origin is unknown.

The shorter, northern branch is at least 82 meters long, with 6 *ojos,* as measured to the edge of the riverbed; it may be of tunneled construction. Informants say that the puquio is not cleaned under the riverbed, but that it does extend to the other side. González García (1934: 218) noted the presence of an *ojo* in the riverbed itself, indicating clearly that this branch does pass below the riverbed. (Rossel Castro [1977: 189-190] adds that this *ojo* was 5.5 meters deep, giving us the depth of the phreatic layer beneath the riverbed. However, his data are so precise here that, like elsewhere, we suspect he was using data from the unpublished version of González García's report.)

The output of Majoro is good, and was relatively higher at the time of González García's study. He noted at the time that it was one of the best maintained of all the puquios, it was cleaned every year, and the *ojos* were lined with wood and kept closed. At present, while the puquio is generally well maintained, it had not been cleaned in some years at the time we recorded it in 1986. And as the branch beneath the bed of the Tierras Blancas River is no longer cleaned, this may account for somewhat reduced flow at present.

The name of the puquio may mean "place of thickets."

Majorito

The puquio Majorito (also called Majoro Chico) is located to the south of the Tierras Blancas River, just east of the puquio Majoro, 3.5 kilometers southwest of Nasca (figure 6.2). It is a trench type puquio, flowing generally northeast to south-

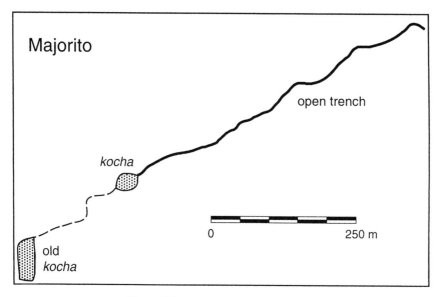

Figure 6.2 Plan of the puquio Majorito.

west. It had a *kocha,* which is still visible, but the *kocha* has not been used in more than thirty years. Instead, the water is diverted out of the trench at a point 251 meters upstream of the original *kocha.* The puquio is open trench its entire length, 823 meters, and it follows a slightly undulating course. At its upper end it bends south, to its origin point which is located just below the lower trench of the Huayrona puquio.

At the time of González García's study the puquio was apparently part open trench and part filled-trench gallery, but he noted that the gallery was in a very poor state of preservation (1934: 218). Since that time, the gallery was dug out, and the puquio left as an open trench. Its output then was quite low, and even today it produces only moderate output.

González García recounts an amusing story of an ingenious way the users of Majorito managed to augment its volume of water some years before his study. The users of the puquio Huayrona undertook to clean the upper portion of that puquio, and they discovered that, while a considerable quantity of water was filtering into and flowing through the gallery, the quantity of water arriving at the *kocha* was much lower in volume. Puzzled, they opened a long stretch of the gallery, seeking the point at which the water was being lost. In doing so they encountered a stone slab in the floor of the gallery through which had been perforated a hole five centimeters in diameter. Water fell through this hole into the puquio Majorito, directly below, robbing Huayrona of much of its water, and augmenting that of Majorito in a most clever, if larcenous, way (González García 1934: 218-219).

Huayrona

The puquio Huayrona is located south of the Tierras Blancas River, just east of Majorito, 2.5 kilometers southwest of Nasca (figure 6.3). It is a trench and gallery type puquio, and it flows southwest then west, then southwest, ending at a *kocha.* The open trench enters the *kocha* at its northeast corner, and it measures 494 meters long. At this point it becomes a filled-trench gallery for 44 meters, then a tunneled gallery for 304 meters more. The filled trench portion was so overgrown that we were not able to see or record any *ojos.* The tunneled portion of the gallery has seven *ojos.* The gallery is said to extend 150 meters beyond the seventh *ojo,* but serious flood damage has occurred since 1944, altering the surface of the land, and obscuring any traces of the puquio. (This damage is probably the result of the narrowing of the riverbed using artificial levees, as the Tierras Blancas River flows through the town of Nasca; see the discussion of Bisambra, above.)

Rossel Castro reported in 1977 (:188-189) that the gallery had interior dimen-

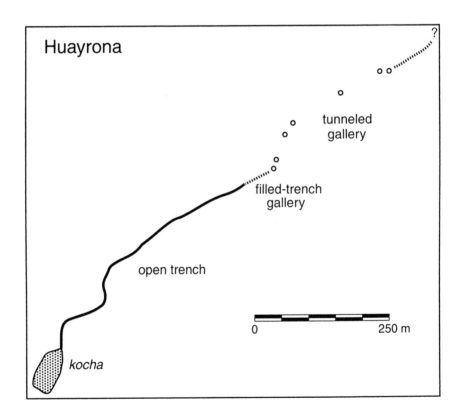

Figure 6.3 Plan of the puquio Huayrona.

sions of 50 cm high and 30 cm wide, and he remarked that it was so small that this must have caused problems for those who needed to enter the gallery to clean it. He then went on to speculate that perhaps this gallery served only a ritual purpose, and it was not meant to be entered. In support of this argument he pointed out the proximity of the puquio to the important site of Kajamarka (Caxamarca; today called Paredones.) However, as we would like to point out, the site of Paredones is actually some 2.5 kilometers east of the puquio, and it is not even within sight of it. We do not accept Rossel Castro's suggestion that this gallery was only of a ritual character; rather, it was probably in a bad state of preservation, and the walls were caving in.

The output of this puquio was very low when measured by González García, but presently it has relatively high output, probably to differences in maintenance.

The name of this puquio derives from the Quechua, *wayra*, which means "wind." The name means "windy place."

San Antonio

The puquio San Antonio (called Pangaraví #1 by earlier writers) is located south of the Tierras Blancas River, southwest of Huayrona, 2 kilometers southeast of Nasca (figure 6.4). It is a trench type puquio, with a tunneled gallery at its upper extreme, flowing generally to the southwest. The open trench enters the *kocha* from the northeast, and it is 488 meters long. Above this point is a slightly depressed area which may indicate a filled-trench gallery, 22 meters long; according to local informants recent excavations revealed a beautifully preserved gallery, but we have not observed this ourselves. There are no obvious *ojos,* but we did observe two depressions that may represent collapsed *ojos.* González García did report one *ojo* (1934: 219).

The output of this puquio is very low, due in part to the lack of natural filtrations this far from either the riverbed or the valley side and in part to the poor maintenance of the puquio. At the time we recorded it, in October of 1986, the water was stagnant at the upper end of the puquio and clogged with algae and aquatic plants. About 50 meters downstream, a sewer line crossing the puquio had broken, and raw sewage was entering the puquio. At present, this is certainly the poorest of the puquios. Interestingly, González García was also of the opinion that this puquio was among the worst of all of the puquios when he did his study (1934: 219.)

San Antonio, along with what we refer to as Pangaraví and Kallanal, watered the hacienda Pangaraví at the time of González García's study. He called the puquios Pangaraví #1, #2 and #3, respectively. He specified that San Antonio watered 54 hectares of the hacienda, and the other two puquios watered the remaining 186 ha of the hacienda.

There is a small Late Intermediate Period site located near the upper end of the puquio.

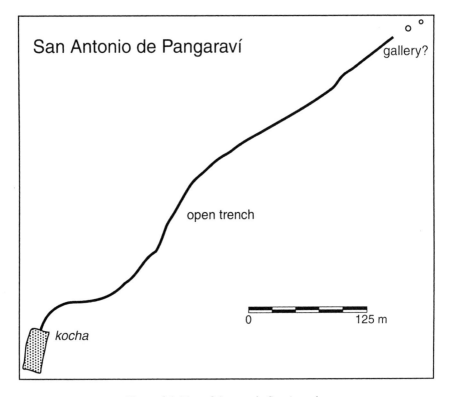

Figure 6.4 Plan of the puquio San Antonio.

Pangaraví

The puquio Pangaraví (called Pangaraví #2 by González García) is located south of the Tierras Blancas River one kilometer south-southwest of Nasca (figure 6.5). It is a trench and filled-trench gallery type puquio with two main branches, one flowing west, the other north. The *kocha,* which lies immediate west of the Pan American Highway, has two chambers and cement walls. The open trench enters from the east, passing under the roadway, and along the southern margin of the barrio of San Carlos; the trench measures 262 meters long to the point where the two branches join. The branch that enters from the south is open trench its entire length of 256 meters. A few hundred meters southeast is found the Inca site of Paredones, formerly called Caxamarca; the filtration zone of this puquio would have provided a convenient supply of domestic water for the settlement.

The second branch continues straight on to the east from the confluence, and it is open trench for 292 meters, at which point it continues as a gallery of filled-trench type construction, 207 meters long; there are five *ojos* along the gallery section.

Rossel Castro believed that this branch of Pangaraví was connected to the puquio La Gobernadora by an underground gallery, and that water from La Gobernadora augmented that of Pangaraví (1977: 187). In fact, he believed that the puquios of Santo Cristo, La Gobernadora, Bisambra, and Pangaraví were all interconnected (1942: 199-200). There is no evidence, however, that any of the puquios are interconnected, and the users of the puquios all agree that each one is independent.

While the output of Pangaraví was relatively high at the time of González García's study, presently its output is relatively low. This is due primarily to the poor state of conservation in which the puquio is found. The main trench and northern branch that pass along the margin of the barrio San Carlos are used as public bathrooms and for garbage disposal.

There are numerous Late Intermediate Period artifacts along the berm near the confluence of the two branches. Near the upper end of the south branch, on its west berm, are artifacts pertaining to the Early Intermediate Period, phases 5-6. This suggests that the puquio Pangaraví existed at that time.

The name of this puquio may translate to mean "festival of maize."

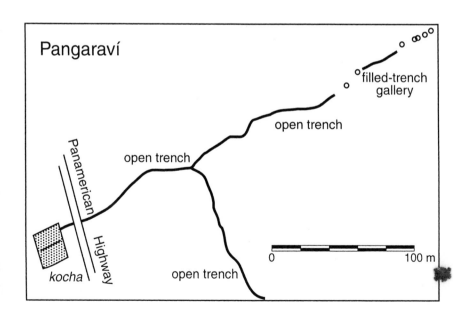

Figure 6.5 Plan of the puquio Pangaraví.

Kallanal

The puquio Kallanal is located along the south margin of the Tierras Blancas River, and it lies within Nasca and the San Carlos barrio; it was called Pangaraví #3 by González García, and it is sometimes known by the name Ramírez. Because the majority of this puquio lies beneath the streets and houses of the barrio San Carlos, we were not able to map it in as great a detail as other puquios. We have estimated the length of the puquio based on aerial photographs. Rossel Castro wrote that this puquio was the least known of all the puquios (1942: 199; 1977: 187); we agree with his assessment. Fortunately, much of the gallery of this puquio was cleaned during the 1986 CORDEICA project, so we have a good eyewitness account of its trajectory, as far as it was cleaned. Like us, the CORDEICA crew did not attempt to map this puquio.

Kallanal has no *kocha* at present, and it did not have one at the time of earlier studies, so perhaps it never had one. Its lower course has been cut by the modern route of the Pan American Highway, so we cannot know its original length. What is visible today is an open trench some 80 meters long, which then continues as a gallery. Because the surface has been completely modified, we cannot say whether it was of filled trench or tunneled construction. Except for the first *ojo,* all have been modified and lined with metal or cement, and they now resemble wells (*pozos*) or manholes (*buzones*).

As the gallery extends up toward the northeast there is visible the one typical *ojo* and one *buzon* in the open area before it passes beneath modern structures. It follows a course toward the northeast with seven more *ojos,* at which point a branch enters from the north. The length of this branch is unknown, but it said to begin under the bed of the Tierras Blancas River; its route is marked by one *ojo* in an open area. The main gallery continues to the northeast, with six more *ojos,* then bends to the east, parallel to the riverbed. This is land reclaimed by artificial levees, and originally this section of the puquio lay beneath the south margin of the riverbed itself. This section continues on, with three more *ojos,* to pass beneath the new bridge that connects Nasca with San Carlos. A short branch, 8 meters long, enters from the right. The CORDEICA project did not clean the puquio beyond this point, owing to a shortfall of funds. The total length of gallery to this point we estimate to be at least 370 meters.

It is clear that the gallery continues some distance more, turning again to the northeast, under the bed of the Tierras Blancas River. It is said that it passes beneath the old municipal market and beyond to pass below the Plaza de Armas of Nasca. This was reported also by Rossel Castro (1977: 188).

The output of this puquio is relatively low, worse than at the time of González García's study, owing probably to the lack of maintenance and cleaning. This puquio has actually caused difficulties for some of the residents of the barrio, as the *ojos* occur on private property, and thieves can enter by crawling through the gallery and up through the *ojos.* One family, with an *ojo* inside their house, reported that they had been robbed in just this manner. At the time of the CORDEICA cleaning, many property owners objected to the presence of strangers, and they tried to prevent the cleaning of the puquio.

The name of this puquio translates to mean "place of the little parrots."

La Gobernadora

The puquio La Gobernadora is located south of the Tierras Blancas River, one kilometer southeast of Nasca (figures 6.6 and 6.7; see also figure 3.10). It is a

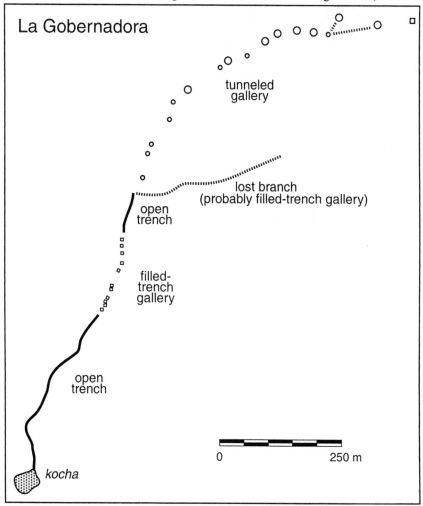

Figure 6.6 Plan of the puquio La Gobernadora.

Figure 6.7 Aerial photograph of La Gobernadora taken in March 1970. The lower end of the puquio is open trench ending at a small *kocha,* visible near the lower left corner of the photograph. The middle section of the puquio is filled-trench gallery; portions have caved in and been left as open trench. The upper section of the puquio is tunneled gallery. Traces of an abandoned second branch may be seen just below (south of) the path that forms the field line running east-west to the right of the puquio. (Photo: SAN.)

trench and gallery type puquio, flowing generally west then southwest; the upper-most end is formed by two short branches. Its *kocha* has not been improved and lined with cement like so many others, and it is one of the few that still remains in somewhat original condition (at least at this writing). The open trench enters the *kocha* at its northeast corner, and it extends 180 meters to the point where it continues as filled-trench gallery. In some parts of this section the fill has been re-moved and short stretches of the gallery are left open; the filled-trench gallery measures 124 meters; the northern branch then continues as tunneled gallery for another 372 meters, with 17 *ojos.* The *ojos* are used by residents of the nearby *barrio* "Santa Fe" as public latrines.

Rossel Castro provides us with an eyewitness account of the interior of the gallery of La Gobernadora: "When I entered the gallery through one of the *ojos*, I was able to see that this was a puquio actually in use, with side walls of stone, and ceiling beams of huarango poles, whose bark is carbonized in order to preserve it from the humidity, and the base of the gallery over which flow the waters is likewise lined with trunks of that tree; despite so many years of having water flow over them they remain shiny, and they seem as though they might have been put there yesterday. The gallery measures 70 cm high by 50 or 60 cm wide" (Rossel Castro 1942: 198-199). The uppermost portion of the puquio is formed by two short branches, as noted by González García (1934: 219).

On 1944 aerial photos there are visible traces of a southern branch, of filled-trench type construction, with about a dozen closely spaced *ojos,* no longer in use. This branch is a continuation of the filled-trench portion of the puquio. The surface of the land was quite uneven in 1944, and there are numerous traces of trenches and berms. Immediately to the southeast, parallel to La Gobernadora, are traces of what may be another puquio entirely, or at least an attempt to build one.

Rossel Castro believed that La Gobernadora was connected to one that he called Kajuka (see Santo Cristo, below). We were told by Sr. Sebastián Jacinto Montoya, a worker who had retired from the hacienda Cantalloq, that before 1944 there was an extension of the right branch that reached toward the sector called Kajuka to the southeast, but because it captured very few filtrations and it took up much arable land, the hacienda owners decided to eliminate it and convert the land into agricultural fields. We suspect that he refers to the now-defunct southern branch.

At the time of his study, González García wrote that this puquio was in the worst condition of all, and that there was an obstruction causing the water to back up and overflow out of the *ojos* onto the land. Since that time, however, that puquio has been well maintained; the land has been leveled so there exist none of the traces visible on 1944 photos. The output of the puquio is only moderate, perhaps owing to its location some distance from the riverbed.

Santo Cristo

The puquio Santo Cristo is located south of the Tierras Blancas River, wrapping around an impervious bedrock outcrop that forms a hill extending into the valley from its south flank, 2.25 kilometers southeast of Nasca (figure 6.8; see also figure 3.11). It is a trench and filled-trench gallery type puquio that has been modified considerably in modern times. The *kocha* is large and lined with cement. The open trench enters the *kocha* from its southwest corner, follows the south valley margin east, then wraps north and east around the end of the hill. The open trench measures 301 meters long, to the point at which it becomes a filled-trench gallery that curves around the hill to the southeast and south. The 8 *ojos* of the gallery are

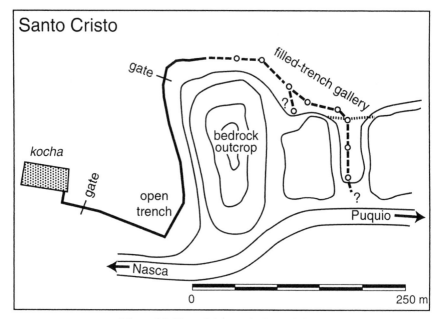

Figure 6.8 Plan of the puquio Santo Cristo.

all cement tubes, and we assume that the gallery itself is also lined with cement tubes; this type of modification is also seen on two puquios in the Las Trancas Valley, Kopara and Chauchilla. The gallery measures 220 meters long.

Rossel Castro reported a possible lost, buried puquio in this location, which he called Kajuka, noting that adjacent to the hill there grew plants that were found only in humid conditions. He also believed that this puquio passed under Cantalloq to La Gobernadora, merging with its puquio and that of Bisambra (Rossel Castro 1942: 198-199), as discussed above. Inspection of 1944 aerial photographs suggests that the puquio existed at the time, and it was an open trench. There is a short second branch near its upper end, entering from the east The present *kocha* did not exist, but a small one may have been located near the end of the outcropping. If the puquio was poorly maintained, it may not have been functioning clearly at the time Rossel Castro made his observations. It is interesting that González García did not record this puquio either.

According to our informant, Sr. Sebastián Jacinto Montoya, sometime around 1944 or 1945 the Negociación Agrícola Cantallo decided to rescue this puquio, which until then was known as the "Puquio Perdido" ("Lost Puquio"), visible only as a thicket of reeds, indicating the presence of subsurface water. The puquio was cleaned out by digging a very deep, narrow trench to find the filtrations, but it could not be left this way without being in constant danger of cave-ins. They therefore decided to lay 24" cement tubes in the trench, and fill it in, using tubes also as vertical *ojos* to provide access into the puquio.

Cantalloq

The puquio Cantalloq (spelled Kantaillo by Rossel Castro in 1942) is located adjacent to the south bank of the Tierras Blancas River, 2.5 kilometers east of Nasca (figures 6.9 and 6.10). It is a trench and gallery type puquio, with two main branches, and it may be the only puquio of primarily tunneled construction. Its *kocha* is today reinforced with cement, and the former hacienda buildings are located immediately adjacent to the *kocha;* these have recently been turned into a hotel for tourists. The open trench enters the *kocha* from the east, and it measures a short

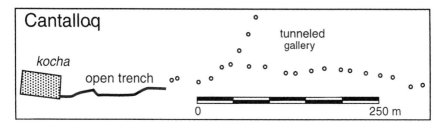

Figure 6.9 Plan of the puquio Cantalloq.

Figure 6.10 Oblique aerial photograph of the puquio Cantalloq. Visible are the two branches, one parallel to the riverbed, the other passing beneath it, that join and eventually empty into an open trench. The kocha is not visible in this photograph.

102 meters long. Above this point it is gallery of tunneled construction, that continues another 104 meters, with six *ojos;* at the sixth *ojo* the two branches join (figure 6.11). The branch from the northeast extends 71 meters and has three more *ojos;* it extends under the bed of the Tierras Blancas River an unknown distance. The branch that continues on to the east is 265 meters long, with 13 *ojos.*

An eyewitness account of the interior of the puquio was given to González García (1934: 221), by the same Vicente Suárez Cervantes who described to him the interior of Bisambra. He reported that in the year 1882 he was contracted for the cleaning of Cantalloq, and at eight in the morning, provided with a candle, a pack of cigarettes, matches, and a bottle of aguardiente, he entered the gallery. At a distance of 130 meters he encountered the first branch, entering from the left, and he continued straight ahead down the main (southern) branch. Many meters farther along he encountered another branch, an unknown branch, entering from the right. He continued straight ahead toward the end of the puquio. About seven or eight blocks (700-800 meters?) farther along the candle went out, and no matter how many times he tried to light it, it only went out again. But he continued on, in the dark. At the end of the gallery he found a large rock, around whose edges filtered a small quantity of water, as it did through the walls and ceiling of the gallery for some distance before the end. The gallery, whose walls began at the edges of the rock, was of variable height and width; in some sections it was pos-

Figure 6.11 The *ojo* of the puquio Cantalloq where the two branches join; author Schreiber is seated near the bottom of the *ojo.*

sible to pass freely walking, and in others it was necessary to crawl through on one's side. He also reported that the quantity of water flowing through the gallery gradually decreased in volume the closer he got to the end, such that only a small thread of water was flowing at its very beginning. He believed the origin of the gallery lay at about 15 meters below the surface of the land. He emerged at six in the evening, nearly asphyxiated; those on the outside believed he had died.

The puquio Cantalloq provides good evidence for the changes in the number of *ojos* over the years. When first recorded by González García, he said that there were three *ojos* in the lower gallery, one *ojo* in the northern branch, and two in the southern branch: a total of six *ojos*. In 1977 (but based on data collected thirty-five years earlier), Rossel Castro wrote that there were fourteen *ojos* along this puquio, which is about the number visible on aerial photographs taken in 1944. On photos taken in 1970 there are visible six *ojos* in the lower gallery, three in the north branch, and eleven in the south branch: a total of twenty *ojos*. Since that date, two new *ojos* have been excavated in the south branch, of rectangular rather than circular form, bringing the total number of *ojos* in this puquio to twenty-two. According to local informants, new *ojos* are built during the cleaning of the puquio, especially in the case of a cave-in blocking the gallery. It is much safer to approach the blockage from above, despite the added labor of excavating a new *ojo*, than to clean the blockage from inside the gallery.

As a result, the *ojos* of the tunneled gallery puquios are today much more closely and evenly spaced than they were in the past. It is possible that at the time of construction of the puquio tunnels there were no *ojos* at all—although one shudders to imagine what excavating and cleaning tunneled galleries must have been like without *ojos*. The construction of *ojos* may be a largely modern occurrence.

Further modification of the *ojos* of the northern branch and the lower puquio occurred during the 1986 CORDEICA project, when a number of the *ojos* were refurbished. The retaining walls in the *ojos* were rebuilt in such a way as to create a spiraling walkway down into the *ojos*, so that tourists and other people could appreciate the puquio (figure 6.12). At this writing, these *ojos* are in a good state of preservation, and the spiral retaining walls well maintained. However, it should be noted that there is no evidence that such a spiraling arrangement was ever characteristic of any *ojos*; this form was an innovation created in 1986.

In the case of Cantalloq, informants report that the gallery is cleaned to a point about 40 meters above the uppermost *ojo* of the south branch, but that the gallery continues some unknown distance beyond that point. If it ever became necessary to clean the puquio to a greater depth, for example, if an extended drought should cause the phreatic layer to drop significantly, we should expect new *ojo* construction along its upper course.

The puquio Cantalloq, like that of Bisambra, figures importantly into local beliefs and legends about water. In part this is due to its proximity to Cerro Blanco the enormous sand-covered sacred mountain that towers above the Nasca Valley Local belief has it that the source of puquio water is a subterranean lake inside

Figure 6.12 Oblique aerial photograph showing newly refurbished *ojos* of the puquio Cantalloq with spiral retaining walls. The original state of the *ojos* can be seen in the other branch of the puquio.

Cerro Blanco, and each year offerings are made on its summit to ensure the rising of the water level in the puquios (Reinhard 1986: 16-20).

One tale that connects the puquio Cantalloq with Cerro Blanco recounts that a worker cleaning the interior of the gallery emerged after many hours at its end, finding himself in a grove of orange trees on the far side of Cerro Blanco An old woman lived in a shack there, and invited him for lunch. When he left she gave him four (or five, depending on the version of the story) oranges. He returned through the puquio to the hacienda and gave the oranges to the owner. The next morning the oranges had turned to gold, and the worker had disappeared, never to be heard from again.

Mojadal—A Possible Lost Puquio

In the Tierras Blancas Irrigation Sector, immediately south of the lower end of the puquio Majoro, is a group of low hills that sit at the original valley edge. (Modern technology now allows cultivation of land to the south of these hills, on land that could not have cultivated using traditional technology.) As we have shown elsewhere, an impervious outcropping that extends into the valley floor may cause a damming effect of the phreatic layer, resulting in a concentration of subsurface water at such locations; it may also be associated with a geologic fault directing water toward the valley. The prehistoric inhabitants understood this association between such valley-side hills and the presence of water, and they built a puquio in nearly every such location. The Majoro hills would seem to be a similar situation. Some years ago the quantity of water at this location was so abundant that it was given the name of El Mojadal. Here plants are found growing that normally exist only in humid conditions. While there is no puquio here at present, there is a long shallow trench exactly where one would expect to find a puquio (figure 6.13). Inspection of the 1944 aerial photographs reveals the presence of this trench, larger and deeper than at present, possibly the remains of a puquio that had fallen out of use by that time. The presence of subsurface water is attested to by the presence of a well immediately adjacent to the trench, up against the edge of the hills. We think it very likely that a puquio once existed at this location, but that it has been out of use for more than a half century.

Figure 6.13 Oblique photograph of the remains of a trench near the hills of Majoro, possibly the location of a puquio, Mojadal.

CHAPTER 7

PUQUIOS OF THE TARUGA
IRRIGATION SECTOR

The Taruga River is a southern tributary of the Rio Grande de Nasca drainage and is located immediately to the south of the Nasca Valley. There is no town at present, although in the portion of the Taruga Valley served by puquios there is a small settlement at Pajonal Alto and an agricultural cooperative at Santa Maria (the former hacienda Taruga). Because the available published version of González García's report does not include this valley, we have no data from 1934 from which to draw comparisons.

The portion of the Taruga Valley served by puquios falls within the Taruga Irrigation Sector as defined by the Peruvian Ministerio de Agricultura. There are presently only two puquios functioning in the Taruga Valley, Santa María and San Carlos, although there was at least one more puquio in this valley in times past, called Camotal (figures 7.1 and 7.2). Another lost puquio was reported upstream

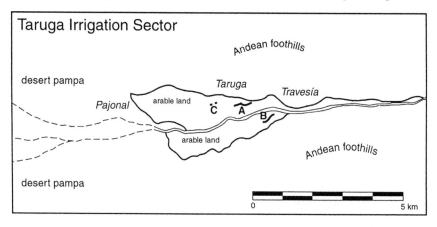

Figure 7.1 Map of the Taruga Irrigation Sector showing limits of arable land, the riverbed, and locations of puquios: A. Santa María, B. San Carlos, and C. the former puquio Camotal.

117

Figure 7.2 Aerial photograph of the puquios of the Taruga Valley taken in March 1970, indicating the locations of the puquios. In the upper left can be seen the ruins of a large Late Nasca town. (Photo: SAN.)

of the others at Travesía, but an investigation of that part of the valley in 1994 turned up no traces of such a puquio. While the Taruga Valley has the least amount of arable land of the three valleys in which puquios are located, its extent was even more limited in prehistoric times, due in part to the peculiarities of the subsurface hydrology. As in the Nasca Valley, the river drops below the surface in the lower Andean foothills, filtering into the alluvial-colluvial fill near the desert plain. In the zone in which puquios are found the phreatic layer is located at a depth of up to 10 meters below the surface. However, rather than rising again gradually to intersect the land some distance downstream, the phreatic layer seems to drop off suddenly to depths of 30 meters or more, judging by the depths of modern wells. These greater depths were apparently beyond the technological skill of the prehistoric inhabitants, who could not build puquios more than about 10 meters deep. The Taruga River emerges again at the surface at an elevation of about 400 m asl, as in the Nasca Valley, except that it does so in multiple small channels, rather than in a single well-defined river course. As a result, the extent of arable land in the Taruga is only about 4 kilometers long, and only a handful of puquios watered this land.

As we have discussed, we believe that this valley may have been included in the study made by González García in 1934, however, the data were not included in the published version of that report. The first reference to puquios in this valley comes to us from the field notes of the American anthropologist-archaeologist Alfred Kroeber, who undertook investigations in the Nasca region in 1926. In his field notes he wrote: "It was said that twenty-eight puquios had been located and cleaned out in the past year (1925) on hacienda Taruga, upstream from it" (Kroeber and Collier 1998: 83). (Note that what he refers to as "puquios" are certainly *ojos.*) His description refers to the puquio now called Santa María.

Mejía Xesspe mentioned only one puquio in this valley, the Pukyo de Taruga (Mejía Xesspe 1939: 562-563), again probably the puquio Santa María. In 1942 Rossel Castro wrote that there were three puquios in this valley, one on the right (north), two on the left (south); in 1977 he wrote in the text that there were two galleries, but on his map he showed three, arranged as described in 1942 (Rossel Castro 1942: 202; 1977: 171, 194).

Santa María

The puquio Santa María is located north of the Taruga River, and it is located on the cooperative of the same name (figure 7.3; see also figure 3.8). It is a trench and filled-trench gallery type puquio, flowing generally from east to west, with two branches. The *kocha* is large and cement-lined. The open trench enters the *kocha* from the east and measures 219 meters long. Above this point it continues as filled-trench gallery for 169 meters, with seventeen preserved *ojos,* to the point where the two branches join; sections of this gallery are poorly preserved, and the

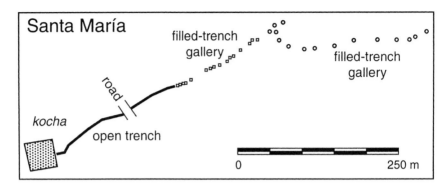

Figure 7.3 Plan of the puquio Santa María.

original number of *ojos* was certainly higher. At this point the gallery is 5.9 meters deep; it was not possible to measure its depth at any higher (deeper) point, but we estimate the maximum depth of this puquio to be on the order of 10 meters.

The short branch that enters from the northeast is of filled-trench construction, and measures 23 meters long, with two *ojos*. The longer branch, which continues on to the east is filled-trench gallery for 256 meters, but has twelve large, conical *ojos*. *Ojos* of this sort usually signal a gallery made by tunneling, however the large berms that flank the puquio along its entire length indicate that it was originally an open trench. This puquio is quite deep, which may account for the large, conical *ojos*. Indeed, a number of the *ojos* in the long branch of this puquio have small cribbed *ojos* built inside the lower half of what appear on the surface as large conical *ojos*.

Mejía Xesspe observed this puquio in July of 1927, and since this is the first detailed eyewitness account of a puquio written by a scientific observer, we include his words here:

> In July of 1927 we visited this valley [Taruga] at the time that they were repairing this aqueduct. There, very close to the hacienda house, we were able to study the structure of the puquio, which was as follows: a horizontal canal flows from east to west, built with large rocks and huarango trunks, whose interior gallery measures 1.20 cm [sic] in height by 0.80 cm wide; the floor is covered with large stone slabs; the side walls are well made with cut stones and some round stones, and in the first courses are left apertures through which the water can filter into the gallery; the ceiling is completely covered with great stone slabs and between them trunks of huarango saturated with humidity, so hard and resistant it is as if they were put there recently. Above the roof is a fill of gravel and soil about three meters thick, and on top grow corpulent huarango and sauce

(*Salix humboldtiana*) trees.
At 30 meters above the profile described we find an "ojo",
a vertical ventilation tube, of quadrangular form, whose characteristics are the following: walls built of large and small stones,
intercalated with huarango trunks to reinforce the wall; small
openings are left along the tube to serve as footholds for the
ascent or descent of those charged with cleaning and conserving
the puquio; the interior dimensions of the tube are 0.60 by 0.80
cm, by a height variable between 3 and 8 meters. The entrance
to the tube is protected by a palisade of huarango sticks, and in
certain cases a kincha wall or an enclosure of spiny shrubs. (Mejía
Xesspe 1939: 562-563)

In the berm near the uppermost *ojos* are seen artifacts pertaining to the late
Middle Horizon Period and Late Intermediate Period. These likely represent a
small occupation on the raised level of the berm, and they indicate that the puquio
was in use at that time.

San Carlos

The puquio San Carlos is located south of the Taruga River, opposite and slightly
upstream of the puquio Santa María (figure 7.4). It is a trench and filled-trench
gallery type puquio, flowing generally from northeast to southwest. The *kocha* is
partially lined with cement, and at its lower end a date of July 18, 1959, is written.
There is an excavation immediately adjacent to the *kocha* to the south that appears
to be a second *kocha*, but it is not currently in use. The open trench enters the
kocha from the east, and is only 66 meters long before it becomes filled-trench
gallery. This portion of the gallery is not in a good state of preservation, and
sections of fill have fallen in and been left open. It is 141 meters long, with thir-
teen small square *ojos* preserved; the original number was certainly much higher.
The upper portion of the puquio measures 184 meters in length; like Santa María it
has large conical *ojos*, but it is flanked with a large berm of soil, indicating that
originally it was built as an open trench.
    Each time we have observed this puquio (in 1986, 1990, and 1995) it has been
nearly or completely dry.

Camotal: An Abandoned Puquio

The puquio Camotal, now abandoned, is located north of the Taruga River, 1 kilometer west of Santa María. All that is visible today are the remains of an open
trench some 425 meters long, flanked by berms that increase in size as one moves

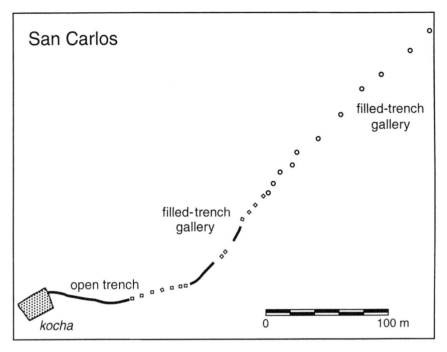

Figure 7.4 Plan of the puquio San Carlos.

upward. No evidence of a *kocha* is visible, and on 1944 aerial photographs the puquio appears to empty directly into the system of *acequias*. Above the trench is an area of wet, saturated ground that may be a small aquifer that was tapped by this puquio; alternatively, it may be water backed up in a hidden gallery that is now blocked.

Informants say this puquio has not been used in some decades, but that it did function within living memory.

Camotal lies directly in front of a large archaeological site (N90-10, Taruga) dating to Late Nasca times, and it could have provided a handy and reliable source of domestic water for the site. The land around the puquio and in front of the site is watered by the puquio Santa María. There are several other sites in the valley that would have depended almost entirely on these puquios for their irrigation and domestic water, including a large settlement at Pajonal Alto (Conlee 2000); that site was occupied from the Middle Horizon through the Inca occupation.

Lost Puquios

Two other puquios, now destroyed, have been reported in this valley: Tres Estrellas, just above San Carlos, and Travesía, located farther upstream. We have been able to find no traces of these lost puquios, but Rossel Castro's map shows a puquio where Tres Estrellas should have been (1977: 171).

CHAPTER 8

PUQUIOS OF THE LAS TRANCAS IRRIGATION SECTOR

The Las Trancas Valley is the southernmost tributary of the Rio Grande de Nasca drainage. As in the Taruga Valley, there are no formal towns, but there are small settlements at Chauchilla and Santa Luisa, and agricultural cooperatives on what were formerly the haciendas of Kopara and Las Trancas. Proportionally, more puquios have been destroyed in this valleys than elsewhere.

The portion of the Las Trancas Valley that is served by puquios falls within the Las Trancas Irrigation Sector, as defined by the Ministerio de Agricultura (figure 8.1). Today there are five functioning puquios in this valley: Chauchilla, Kopara, El Pino, Pampón, and Totoral. Of those, Chauchilla and Kopara have been substantially modified in recent decades. In the past there were at least eight puquios in this valley: La Joya was destroyed some decades ago, and Huaquilla Chica and Huayurí have been converted into *pozo-kochas*. There may have been

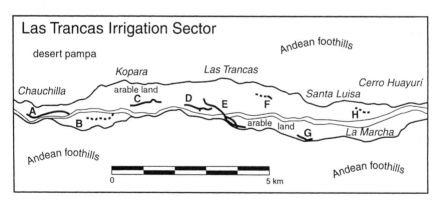

Figure 8.1 Map of the Las Trancas Valley showing limits of arable land, the dry riverbed, and locations of current and former puquios: A. Chauchilla; B. La Joya; C. Kopara; D. El Pino; E. Pampón; F. Huaquilla Chica; G. Totoral; H. Huayurí.

three or more additional puquios in this valley in the past.

The Las Trancas Valley has a gradient that is slightly gentler than that of the Nasca and Taruga valleys, as the land drops in elevation from east to west. As a result, the puquios in this valley tend to be longer, on average, than those of the other valleys.

The first scientific reference to the puquios in this valley is found in the 1926 field notes of Alfred Kroeber. He wrote that, "Las Trancas . . . is said to have a system of eighty [*ojos*], long in use" (Kroeber and Collier 1998: 83). He does not, however, provide us with any eyewitness accounts of puquios in this valley.

Our most complete data for this valley come from Mejía Xesspe, who named and described six puquios that he observed in 1927. He provided a rough sketch map of the valley, showing the approximate locations of the puquios he studied. This is fortunate because Mejía Xesspe's data, while the most detailed of the published sources for this valley, are very difficult to work with, and it is a challenge to correlate the puquios he described in 1927 with those that exist today. The names he gave for the puquios are either confused, or the names have changed; the sketch plan of the valley does help sort out the confusion somewhat but does not resolve the entire problem. We have been able to identify with certainty only four of the six puquios he described: El Pino, Pampón, Totoral, and Huayurí, which he called Pukyo E (unnamed), Pukyo D (Totoral), Pukyo B (La Marcha), and Pukyo A (Pukyo Perdido), respectively. For his remaining two puquios we can only determine the general area in which each puquio was located. His Pukyo F (unnamed) was located approximately on the hacienda Kopara, which had three puquios: Chauchilla, La Joya, and Kopara. And his Pukyo C (Pampón) is probably the puquio we call Huaquilla Chica, but we cannot be absolutely certain of this identification.

Rossel Castro wrote in 1942 that there were eight puquios functioning in this valley. In 1977 he described six, said there were seven, but noted eight on his sketch map (Rossel 1942: 201, 1977: 169, 171, 191-194). He describes Pampón in some detail, given its peculiar architecture (1977: 191-194).

Chauchilla

The puquio Chauchilla is located north of the Las Trancas River, and it waters the lands of the same name; also called Canales, it may be Mejía Xesspe's Pukyo F. On 1944 aerial photographs it is visible as a long open trench, with a possible gallery at its upper end near the riverbed; it had a *kocha* (figure 8.2). Today the puquio appears on the surface only as a line of what appear to be small wells (figure 8.3). The puquio was lined with cement tubes and filled, and *ojos* were created with cement tubes. A large cement reservoir stands at the approximate location of the original *kocha*. We have not mapped this puquio in detail, since at the time of our field study we did not realize that it still functioned. We estimate its

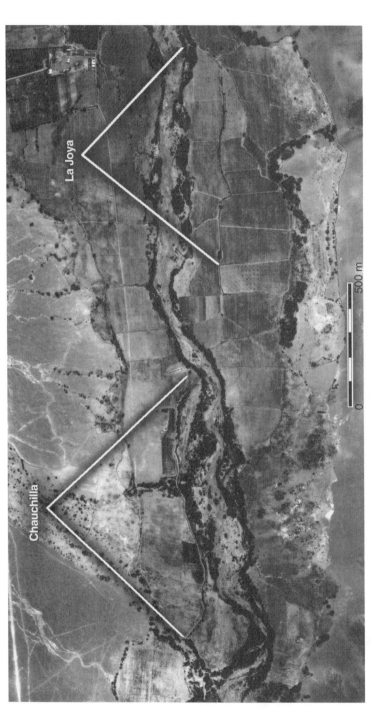

Figure 8.2 Aerial photograph of the puquios Chauchilla and La Joya taken in December 1944. Chauchilla is seen as a large open trench leading to a *kocha* at the left margin of the photograph; the upper end reaches just to the riverbed. The puquio La Joya is seen to the east, south of the riverbed; clearly visible is the *kocha*, open trench, and gallery section curving northward to the riverbed. (Photo: SAN.)

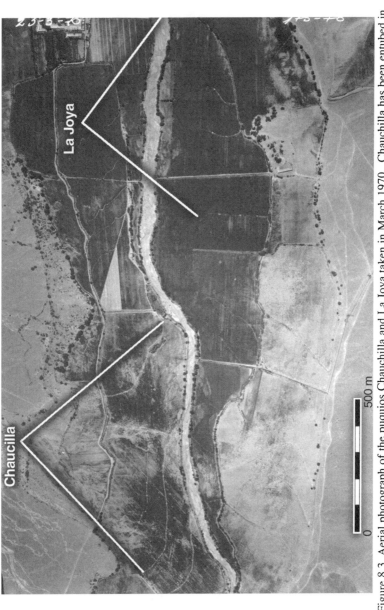

Figure 8.3 Aerial photograph of the puquios Chauchilla and La Joya taken in March 1970. Chauchilla has been entubed in cement and all that is visible at the surface is a line of cement tube wells, each less than one meter in diameter. The La Joya puquio has been completely destroyed. (Photo: SAN.)

length to be on the order of 1,280 meters.

We had the good fortune to speak with Sr. Donato Salguero, tambero of the cooperative Tupac Amaru, at the former hacienda Kopara, who lived on this land since 1935, when he came there at the age of fifteen. He was able to give us descriptions of the three puquios that formerly watered this hacienda, one of which has since been destroyed (La Joya) and two extensively modified (Chauchilla and Kopara). According to him, the puquio found in the region of Chauchilla was called Canales by the tenant farmers there. It began as a gallery on the south margin of the riverbed, crossing diagonally (northwest) to the other side and continuing on to its *kocha;* this conforms to what is visible on 1944 aerial photographs. He said that its output was 40 liters per second.

La Joya—A Destroyed Puquio

The puquio La Joya, now destroyed, was located south of the Las Trancas River, on the land of the Copara hacienda, between the Chauchilla and Kopara puquios; it may have been Mejía Xesspe's Pukyo F. It is clearly visible on aerial photographs of 1944, but by 1970 was completely gone (see figures 8.2 and 8.3). Originally it had a *kocha,* and an open trench about 750 meters long entered from the west. The uppermost section of the puquio, 150 meters long, is visible as six large *ojos,* turning northeast to the edge of the riverbed. All that is visible on the ground surface today is a higher than normal concentration of stone cobbles along the path of the puquio.

According to our informant, Sr. Donato Salguero, this puquio began on the south margin of the riverbed, and it had two branches. The gallery was manifest by a series of *ojos,* which were used during the cleaning of the puquio. The output of the puquio was 50 liters per second. He went on to say that the output of the puquio was too low, given the amount of land taken up on the surface by the open trench, so the owners of the hacienda simply filled it in. This occurred around 1945 or soon thereafter, about the same time that the other puquios were modified.

Kopara—A Modified Puquio

The puquio Kopara, now entubed in cement like Chauchilla, is located on the lands of the former hacienda, north of the Las Trancas River. It is visible on 1944 aerial photographs as an open trench with *kocha.* At about the same time that the Chauchilla and La Joya puquios were altered, Kopara was entubed in cement and buried. Like Chauchilla, all that is visible on the surface is a line of widely spaced small wells. We were able to measure 478 meters of this puquio in 1988, but we believed it was substantially longer. In the course of doing the archaeological survey in 1996, we located an additional several hundred meters of the puquio.

We have been told that it extends nearly to the former Las Trancas hacienda, but we have never been able to map it in its entirety.

According to our informant, Sr. Donato Salguero, this puquio begins near the *kocha* of the puquio El Pino. It had nine *ojos* and then an open section before arriving at its own *kocha;* it was some 700 meters long. Its output was 50 liters per second, and it was called La Clemencia because a tenant farmer with that name lived very near to it. The puquio was canalized in cement tubes of 24" diameter, and cement tube *ojos,* analogous to traditional *ojos,* were created. In this manner it was possible to fill in the puquio trench, which was more than 10 meters wide, and gain valuable agricultural land.

It is interesting to note the similarities in puquio modification in the cases of Chauchilla and Kopara in the Las Trancas Valley, and Santo Cristo in the Nasca Valley. In both cases the land and puquios were owned by the same brothers, which probably explains the similar treatment of the puquios (not to mention the destruction of La Joya), and the efforts to gain more agricultural land.

El Pino—A Partially Converted Puquio

The puquio El Pino is located parallel to the north bank of the Las Trancas River, just south of the buildings of the former hacienda of Las Trancas (figures 8.4, 8.5, and 8.6); it was called Pukyo E by Mejía Xesspe. It is a trench and gallery type puquio with two branches. We were fortunate to have as our informant, Sr. Martín Copa, the person in charge of the annual cleaning of this and the puquio Pampón. He has been inside the complete length of these puquios, and he was able to provide details we could never have seen ourselves.

The *kocha* of El Pino was built sometime between 1944 and 1970, and we were told that none of the puquios in this part of the valley had *kochas,* originally. The open trench enters from the east, and measures 436 meters long to the point where it becomes filled-trench gallery; below this point a short former branch *(cangrejera)* entered from the south, and it is still marked by a depression in the large berm along the south side of the puquio, but our informant indicated that it

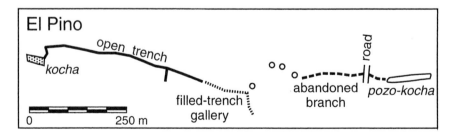

Figure 8.4 Plan of the puquio El Pino.

no longer functions.

The gallery continues on for 123 meters to the point where two branches join. The south branch is 54 meters long and is of filled-trench construction, beginning near the riverbank. Sr. Copa indicated that it does not continue any farther and does not pass under the riverbed, as is common in other puquios.

The longer north branch continues for 238 meters more as filled-trench gallery, bending north and then east again. It is not cleaned any great distance, and as a result, the volume of water from this branch is lower than that of the shorter southern branch. The uppermost section of this puquio, some 123 meters long, has been completely opened up, and it now serves as a *pozo-kocha*. Indeed, the modern users were not aware that it was connected in any way to the puquio, but it is clear on the aerial photographs of 1944 that it was part of the puquio, and it was of filled-trench construction.

Figure 8.5 Aerial photograph of the puquios El Pino and Pampón taken March 1970. The puquio El Pino is seen as an open trench and filled-trench gallery parallel to the riverbed, with a short branch entering from the south. Above this point filled-trench gallery is visible. The uppermost segment of the puquio has been opened up and converted into a *pozo-kocha*. Pampón begins as two filled-trench gallery branches along the valley edge south of the river. Under the riverbed the galleries join and cross to the north side. From this point the filled-trench gallery can be seen; it opens into a trench and empties directly into irrigation canals. (Photo: SAN.)

Figure 8.6 Oblique aerial photograph of the puquio El Pino, looking to the southeast.

Pampón

The puquio Pampón is located along the south side of the valley, beginning south of the Las Trancas River, but crossing to the north side (figure 8.7); it was called Pukyo D by Mejía Xesspe. It has no *kocha,* but empties directly into the system of *acequias.* Our measurements begin at the point where it intersects the first *acequias* as it crosses the road that provides access up the center of the valley.

Pampón begins as an open trench for 280 meters, but very soon it continues as filled-trench gallery. Much of the gallery is poorly preserved, and long sections have been opened up, exposing the gallery (see figure 3.9); the filled-trench gallery extends for 448 meters, angling southeast toward the riverbed. It crosses diagonally under the riverbed a distance of 216 meters (figure 8.8). At this point two branches join; we were only able to map the longer of them, and even our informant had little information about the shorter branch, as it is never cleaned. Rossel Castro provides an eyewitness description of this confluence, saying that the branch entering from the left lay at a higher elevation than the one on the right, and that the water cascaded down a stone staircase where they joined (Rossel 1942: 201; 1977: 193).

We were more fortunate than the users of this puquio when we did our first field study in 1986: there was an obstruction blocking the flow of water in the gallery, causing it to back up and fill many of the *ojos.* Normally the *ojos* in the riverbed are completely invisible, making an accurate map of the trajectory of the

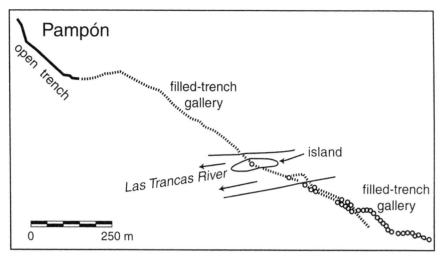

Figure 8.7 Plan of the puquio Pampón.

Figure 8.8 Oblique aerial photograph of the puquio Pampón, viewed to the south. The longer branch approaches from the left, while the shorter branch begins up against the valley side. The two branches join under the riverbed. The puquio is again visible on the lower right as it appears from under the riverbed.

puquio nearly impossible, but we were able to locate two *ojos* in the riverbed because the surface of the ground was saturated with water that had backed up and filled the concealed *ojos.*

The longer branch, which we mapped, follows a path along the valley side for the rest of its length. According to our informant, the shorter branch follows the course of the riverbed, then angles in toward the long branch, parallels it for a distance, and then passes beneath it, and terminates in a natural (?) cul-de-sac in the valley side. We were not able to map this branch ourselves, as there are few surface traces of it that we could see. The plan made by González García, and published by Rossel Castro (1977: 192) shows both branches, but it does not show the branches crossing. Based on what we were told by Sr. Copa, we estimate its length as about 340 meters from the point where it joins the longer branch, under the riverbed.

The long branch, continues along the valley margin for a distance of 536 meters, with two short branches *(cangregeras)* entering from the south; it is of filled-trench construction. We had no trouble mapping this branch, as its twenty-nine *ojos* made it easy to follow.

The uppermost end of the puquio has a structure that may be unique among all the puquios. The gallery suddenly widens to more than 4 meters, and it is 3 meters tall. As our informant expressed it, "It's so big you could fit a Volvo truck in there." This serves as a sort of subterranean reservoir where water collects before it flows down the gallery. The surface of the land over this reservoir exhibits a depression about 6 to 8 meters wide, and 32 meters long.

Flowing into this subterranean reservoir is a short gallery, 9 meters long, that begins at an *"ojo,"* a circular, stone-line pit, which is the exact point at which the water filters into the puquio. Sr. Copa said that it has two chambers, an upper and a lower one, and that the water filters into the lower chamber from its north side (from the river); the water is 10 meters deep. The upper chamber is opened to provide access to the lower chamber at the time of cleaning.

Rossel Castro (1977: 193-194) wrote that a Sr. José Navarro, who was mayor-domo of the hacienda Las Trancas in 1942, had found a prehistoric ceramic vessel in the internal reservoir. The vessel was in the form of a nutria, a type of otter sometimes regarded as sacred in the Andes. From the description of the vessel it seemed to Rossel Castro that it pertained to the Early Nasca culture of the Early Intermediate Period, and that, hence, the puquios also dated to that period. We hesitate to accept his conclusion, based on the evidence he used.

We were interested to note that, in his 1977 chapter, Rossel reproduces several of González García's plans and profiles of the puquios, including one of Pampón. It is this profile of Pampón that first led us to believe that González García actually did study the puquios of the Las Trancas and Taruga valleys, but that only the data from Nasca were published. Rossel Castro's data are so detailed in some cases that he could have been taking them only from an unpublished version of González García's report.

Huaquilla Chica—A Converted Puquio

In the center of the valley floor, about 2.25 kilometers east of the former Las Trancas hacienda, is a natural mound called Huaquilla Chica. On 1944 aerial photographs there was clearly functioning a puquio at this location, probably of open trench and filled-trench construction. It began about 500 meters to the east of the mound and followed along its northern perimeter; there was no *kocha,* and the water entered the system of *acequias* directly. Today all that is left of this puquio is a *pozo-kocha* located at what was the upper end of the puquio. This is probably the puquio that Mejía Xesspe called Pukyo C, which he said was named Pampón.

Totoral

The puquio Totoral is located along the south flank of the valley, south of the Las Trancas River, 4 kilometers east-southeast of the former Las Trancas hacienda (figure 8.9); this is Mejía Xesspe's Pukyo B, which he said was named La Marcha. It has a large cement *kocha,* and the open trench enters from the south side. The open trench is only 96 meters long, and turns east and continues as filled-trench gallery for 468 meters, and as gallery of probable filled-trench construction another 90 meters to its end. Informants report that there are actually two branches of this puquio, but only one is visible on the surface. Portions of the gallery were poorly preserved, and it had been opened up exposing an open trench. We recorded fifty-nine *ojos* in the preserved sections of the gallery, more than in any other puquio, and the original number was certainly much higher.

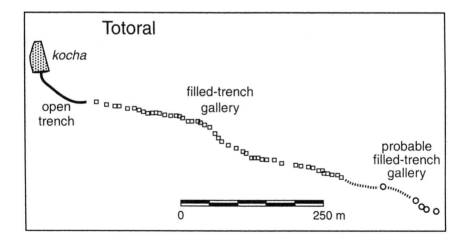

Figure 8.9 Plan of the puquio Totoral.

In one stretch it was clear that the fill over the gallery had been washed away as a result of a particularly damaging river flood. The nearly complete structure of one of the *ojos* was left free-standing and completely exposed. Its cribbed-log structure could be seen in all its detail.

While the puquio follows the valley flank for most of its course, near its lower end it continues straight toward the *kocha,* while the valley flank angles slightly away. The small triangle of valley bottom land in between the puquio and the valley flank was effectively cut off from potential irrigation water by the construction of the puquio (figure 8.10). This is one of the rare instances in which we find a prehistoric site located on valley bottom land; normally sites were located along the valley sides, above any potentially arable land. Because the construction of the puquio trench created a barrier to the passage of irrigation water across the surface of the land, this parcel of land was rendered useless for cultivation; it therefore became suitable for the location of a settlement. The date of such a settlement should give us a date *ante quem* for the construction of the puquio.

The site on this parcel of land, unfortunately, was leveled some decades ago, so there is no visible architecture remaining. The remains still visible include ceramics, lithics, and food remains, indicating probable habitation. The lack of

Figure 8.10 Oblique aerial photograph of the Las Trancas Valley showing the dry riverbed and the limits of cultivation. The puquio Totoral is visible flowing along the valley flank, then continuing into the valley and turning north to its *kocha.* The triangle of land between the lower end of the puquio and the valley edge could not have been irrigated after construction of the puquio.

intensive looting indicates quite clearly that the site was not a cemetery. The artifacts collected at the site by the local residents were shown to us, and all pertain to the Transitional Nasca phase (EIP 5), or roughly about AD 400-500. This suggests that this particular puquio existed at that time.

Huayurí—A Converted Puquio

Clearly visible in the aerial photographs taken in 1944, in the upper portion of the valley, north of the Las Trancas River, and below the sacred mountain, Huayurí, is a puquio of trench and filled-trench gallery type, with no *kocha*. This is probably the puquio that Mejía Xesspe called Pukyo A, the Pukyo Perdido (Lost Puquio) (1939: 560-561). He described it as being an open trench in its lower extent, and a gallery with *ojos* in its upper extent; he calculated its length as about 400 meters.

By 1970 the puquio had been buried, and a portion of it was left open as a *pozo-kocha*. Its present users knew nothing about the old puquio when questioned in 1991. The *pozo-kocha* is called El Limón. There is little surface indication of the uppermost portion of the old gallery, except a greater concentration of river cobbles in the soil than might otherwise be expected. It is possible, however, that filtrations from the old gallery still channel water toward the *pozo-kocha*.

We interviewed one resident of the region who remembered the puquio, Sr. Adolfo Navarro Monge, eighty-three years old (in 1986), who had worked in all parts of this valley between 1917 and 1950. He told us that he had had the great fortune to meet Drs. Julio C. Tello and Toribio Mejía Xesspe when they came to the valley to make their studies in the 1920s. He corroborated the description given by Mejía Xesspe, adding that the puquio was rather poor in water, and that it served to water the *fundo* of Santa Luisa.

In 1995, excavations in the riverbed east of El Limón revealed a segment of stone-lined gallery. This gallery was most likely an extension of the puquio Huayurí.

Lost Puquios

We have no firm evidence for other puquios in this valley, except for traces visible on 1944 aerial photographs. Located at the upper end of valley on the south side at La Marcha, opposite the Huayurí puquio, there are traces of a possible destroyed puquio visible on the 1944 photo. Mejía's Pukyo B (1939: 561), may refer to this puquio, or to Totoral. On the north side of the valley, near the small settlement at Santa Luisa, there is visible on the 1944 air photo a short length of depressed land between two mounds. This looks like the remnants of the upper end of a puquio. It appears that there was a square hole or well dug into the depression, which would support the notion that there was a filled-trench gallery below the surface there. At present one of the mounds has been leveled, and the depression filled, leaving no traces of this possible puquio.

Below Chauchilla the valley floor narrows and there are no settlements, historic or prehistoric, for about 5 kilometers. However, in the vicinity of Poroma there is a sizable Late Intermediate Period occupation, and traces of old agricultural fields visible on the 1944 photos. We suspect there may have been a puquio in this area as well.

Puquios in Other Valleys

We have no evidence at this time for the existence of puquios in any of the other valleys of the Río Grande de Nasca drainage. This is not surprising, given the differences in availability of water between the southern and northern rivers of the drainage, as documented in chapter 2. What we do find in those other river valleys is the excavation of shallow temporary wells during the dry season when the rivers may drop beneath the surface. That is, some of the northern rivers may be influent at certain times of the year, or in certain segments of their valley. However, since those rivers flow fairly consistently and regularly every year during the highland rainy season, and continue to flow nearly year-round, there was little incentive for residents of those valleys to invest the labor necessary to build permanent puquios.

Likewise, in the Ica Valley, the Ica River may be influent at times, especially when irrigation water is being drawn out of it into the major La Chirana irrigation canal. We see no evidence for puquio construction in Ica, however. At present we are not aware of puquios in any other coastal valley that are comparable, especially in date of construction, to those of Nasca. Elsewhere on the coast of Peru and Chile puquio-like constructions do exist, but in most cases these were probably built by the Spanish, as will be discussed below.

CHAPTER 9

THE DATING OF THE PUQUIOS

The puquios have apparently existed for quite some time, but the question we must address is, just how long have they been in use? And who built them? It has been the general consensus of the people of Nasca and the archaeological community that the puquios were built by the prehispanic people of Nasca, but until recently there have been no hard data upon which to base this interpretation. As discussed in chapter 1, there was only one major known autochthonous civilization in the region, the Nasca culture of the Early Intermediate Period. Therefore, most people have regarded the people of this culture as the likeliest candidates for the builders of the puquios. As we have seen, however, this was not the only prehispanic culture to dominate the region, and even within the Early Intermediate Period the Nasca culture underwent a series of significant changes. In this chapter we shall present archaeological evidence for the initial use of the system in the mid-first millennium AD, during the transitional phase 5 of the Early Intermediate Period culture, and its continued use, and probable expansion, up to and including the Inca occupation of 1476-1533. We address recent arguments that the puquios are not an indigenous development, but were rather introduced and built by the Spanish. We will also consider evidence that the Spanish may have added to and modified the existing system of puquios.

Most writers dealing with Nasca and its history are familiar with the puquios, and many have expressed an opinion as to the date of construction of the puquios. Most writers of published works that focus specifically on the Nasca puquios concur that they are prehispanic in date, but differ regarding the culture of their builders. González García (1934) was of the opinion that they were built by the Incas, as indicated by the title of his article: "Los acueductos incaicos de Nazca." With regard to the conservation and improvement of the system, he wrote that to restore the puquios to their original condition would require resources beyond the means of the Peruvian state, and that the value of the entire Nasca Valley was less than the cost of refurbishing the system. In his opinion, the construction of such works could only have been accomplished in the time of the Incas (González García 1934: 221-222).

Mejía Xesspe, on the other hand, was the first scientific writer to suggest that the puquios were built by the Nasca culture or earlier. Their location within an area of a well-defined civilization and their crucial economic function led him to think that they were built by the people of what he termed the Nasca Nation, or else by pre-Nasca people (Mejía Xesspe 1939: 565).

Alberto Regal (1943) indicated his general opinion that the puquios were prehispanic in the title of his article, "Los acueductos precolombinos de Nasca." In the text, moreover, he stated that although earlier works had attributed the puquios to the Incas (probably referring to González García), he could now affirm with relative certainty that they corresponded to earlier epochs. He was of the opinion, like Mejía Xesspe, that the puquios pertained to Nasca or pre-Nasca cultures (Regal 1943: 210-211).

Rossel Castro felt strongly that the puquios were preincaic. He observed that the Incas encountered many wonderful and impressive works in the regions they conquered, and, in their great wisdom, let them continue to operate as before. The century and a half that the Incas dominated Nasca would not, he felt, have been long enough to accomplish such works in this valley (Rossel Castro 1942: 202). In his later work he wrote that the puquios must have been built by what he termed the "Civilización Naska." He based this on the report of the finding of a ceramic vessel in the form of a nutria in the cistern of the puquio Pampón (1977: 193-194), as we have mentioned above.

In more recent decades, the archaeological community has expressed a consensus that the puquios probably pertain to the Nasca culture of the Early Intermediate Period, as noted by Rogger Ravines in a footnote to the reprinted version of González García's article (González García 1978: 130).

Georg Petersen wrote that he was of the opinion that the construction of the hydraulic system began in Middle Nasca times, and ended or was suspended in Late Nasca, at the same time that a site he calls Cahuachi II ceased to exist, more or less between AD 400 and 800 (Petersen 1980: 21). According to his interpretation, there was a climatic crisis that forced people to move from Cahuachi to a new site, Cahuachi II, 20 kilometers upstream; there they began to build the filtration galleries. His Cahuachi II, unfortunately, seems to be the site usually known as Paredones, actually an Inca site, so this interpretation is a bit problematic. However, he does point out that there is no other locality on the coast of Peru where filtration galleries of pre-Columbian age are known to have existed (Petersen 1980: 30).

We find that all these suggestions are reasonable, based upon the evidence available to each writer. However, we now have more direct and detailed data that permit a more precise dating of the construction of the puquios. We find that reliable lines of evidence point to a date of initial construction in EIP phase 5 (Transitional Nasca), or roughly AD 400-500.

The Evidence

There are two primary lines of archaeological evidence that can shed light on the date of construction of the puquios. First, sites in direct association with the puquios should indicate the dates of use of particular puquios, although in some cases such sites may postdate the date of initial puquio construction. Second, shifts in permanent settlement locations away from the upper or lower portions of each valley and into the dry middle valley should be correlated with the development of the system of puquios in general. In addition to these two lines of evidence we also consider iconography and the utility of radiocarbon dating.

Sites in direct association with puquios

As we have seen in the preceding chapters, there are numerous cases in which we find archaeological remains on the berms of the puquios. Although people rarely lived on the arable valley bottom, the excavation of puquio trenches created large elevated berms that were unsuitable for cultivation. Sites found on the berms must necessarily postdate puquio construction, and the date of their occupation indicates a period in which the puquio was in use.

As we have seen in several cases (Soisonguito, Agua Santa, Anglia, Achaco, Curve, San Antonio, Pangaraví, and Santa María), remains from periods as early as the Middle Horizon, and continuing through the Late Intermediate Period and Late Horizon, and even into the Colonial Period, are found on puquio berms. In the case of Pangaraví, artifacts from even earlier periods, Early Intermediate 5-6 (transitional to Late Nasca), are present. While these remains might result from the puquio trenches having been excavated through existing sites, there should be remains visible in the stratigraphy exposed in the trench sides. Careful inspection of visible stratigraphy reveals no such remains to date. There is little evidence for human settlement on the arable valley floor, except on rises of land that cannot be irrigated. Puquio berms form such elevations of land, and are therefore logical places to expect small prehistoric occupations. And indeed, we do find such occupations in a number of cases, indicating the existence of puquios at least as early as the Middle Horizon.

The case of the puquio Totoral also provides evidence for a puquio in use during EIP phase 5 times. As discussed in chapter 8, the creation of this puquio blocked off a segment of valley bottom land such that irrigation water could no longer reach this tract of land; this land therefore became suitable for settlement. A small domestic site was established there in EIP 5 times.

Settlement patterns

Before considering settlement patterns—the distribution of sites throughout the region, and changes in that distribution over time—we must reprise our earlier discussion of the natural environment of the region, and the availability of surface water in different portions of the valley. Given a nearly complete absence of rainfall in Nasca, the availability of surface and subsurface water determines whether or not human settlement was possible in each zone, with or without puquios. In the sierra, rainfall agriculture is possible, and irrigation is not necessary. In the upper valley, irrigation is required, but perennial surface water provides a reliable source. In the zone of infiltration, the rivers may or may not be present on the surface of the land, depending on the season of the year and longer-term climatic patterns. The middle valley is completely dry most or all of the year, and only by tapping the phreatic layer with puquios is this portion suitable for permanent occupation. The lower valley, where the river flows again, can be occupied and irrigated using reliable river water.

If we look at the locations of settlements in these zones, and how those locations changed through time, we can discern specific changes correlated with the development of the system of puquios. We make the following assumptions. First, in periods prior to the time of construction and use of the puquios, permanent habitation sites should be rare to nonexistent in the dry middle valleys. While the land might be irrigated and cultivated during years that the river flowed, most years saw little water in this portion of the valleys, and certainly not a drop following the highland dry season. It is therefore extremely unlikely that permanent habitation sites were established in the dry portions of the valleys in the absence of puquios. However, there would have been no barrier to the establishment of cemeteries in this zone.

Second, in periods prior to puquio construction we should find permanent settlements located in the lower and upper valleys, where perennial water is available, and probably in the zone of infiltration, where water is usually available. As the lower valley is rather inhospitable due to high temperatures and terrible wind storms, we should anticipate finding most habitation in the zone of infiltration and in the upper valley.

Third, after the construction of puquios the middle valley was made habitable year-round; therefore we expect to see a shift in settlement locations into this region correlated with the use of the puquios. In fact, given that there is substantially more arable land in the middle valley, we might expect to see the majority of the population moving into the middle valley as the use of the puquios increased.

Archaeological surveys of the Nasca Valley (including the Aja and Tierras Blancas tributaries), and portions of the Taruga and Las Trancas valleys (Figure 9.1) were undertaken by Schreiber, along with her colleagues and students, between 1985 and 1996 (Schreiber 1987, 1990, 1991; Schreiber and Isla 1995, 1998). Survey was conducted on foot by a crew of three to six persons, and aerial recon-

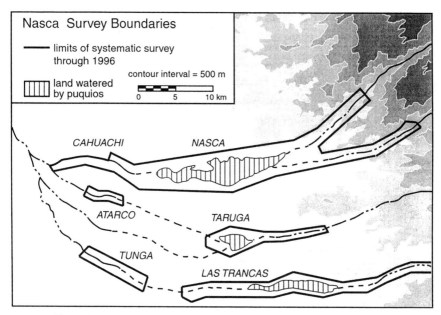

Figure 9.1 Boundaries of the areas systematically surveyed, 1986-1996.

naissance and photography were used to both locate and record sites.

The region comprises four topographic zones with significant differences in density of prehistoric occupation, and which were surveyed at different intensities. These include valley edges, ridges and hilltops, valley bottoms, and desert pampa. Since nearly all sites are located on the valley edges, immediately adjacent to the arable valley bottom, these areas were surveyed 100 percent and hundreds of sites have been located and recorded. In this endeavor it was important to distinguish between the modern valley edge and the prehistoric valley edge, as modern technology has permitted the cultivation of areas beyond the prehispanic limits of the valley bottoms. Ridges and hill tops were surveyed only in the lowest portion of the Andean foothills, up to 250 meters above the valley floor; sites ranging from small ephemeral occupations to fortresses were located on several of these hilltops.

Sites visible in the valley bottom are located only on low rises of land where irrigation water cannot reach; these include natural and man-made mounds, and the berms of puquios. All such areas were surveyed, except where vicious dogs caused us to skirt around some pieces of land, and many show evidence of prehistoric occupation. In addition to these parcels, approximately 25 percent of the arable valley bottom was surveyed in each valley; thus far, no prehistoric settlements have been located on the cultivated land of the valley bottoms. Local farmers report that artifacts are rare to nonexistent in their fields, except around puquios.

Survey of the valley bottom did allow us to define the prehistoric limits of arable land, and hence the prehistoric valley edge. The use of motor-driven pumps, along with the excavation of *pozo-kochas,* has expanded cultivation significantly in some parts of the valleys. The modern valley edge, especially in the Nasca Valley between Soisonguito and Ayapana, lies significantly beyond the prehistoric valley edge.

Survey did not extend away from the valleys onto the desert pampa or far up alluvial fans of side valleys; these areas are covered with geoglyphs and it is prohibited to walk on or near them without special permission. Since the geoglyphs were not a primary focus of our study, such permission was not sought.

Thus far, systematic survey has been completed in the Nasca Valley, beginning near the confluence of the southern tributaries at Tambo de Perro, at an elevation of 300 m asl, up the Aja tributary to an elevation of 1,200 m asl at Asiento, and up the Tierras Blancas tributary to an elevation of 1,600 m asl at Ronquillo, some 60 kilometers from Tambo de Perro. The Taruga valley has been surveyed between the elevations of 550 and 800 m asl, from Pajonal Alto to Ramadayoq, a distance of 12 kilometers. Below 550 m the valley is not well defined topographically, water sources are extremely rare, and the underground river divides and emerges in at least two locations. One of these, Atarco, was also surveyed. The Las Trancas Valley has been surveyed from lower Tunga, at an elevation of 350 m asl, to Isla at 1,200 m asl, a distance of 60 kilometers. Thus in the Nasca (Aja and Tierras Blancas) Valley, and the Las Trancas Valley, the survey includes all four hydrologic sectors below the sierra: upper valley, zone of infiltration, middle valley, and lower valley. In the Taruga Valley systematic survey includes part of the zone of infiltration, the dry middle valley, and part of the lower valley. Thus our overall settlement patterns should provide the lines of evidence necessary to define periods before and after puquio construction.

When we compare settlement patterns of the EIP 2-4 (Early Nasca) Period with those of the Late Intermediate Period (figures 9.2 and 9.3) we clearly see our expected "before" and "after" patterns. In Early Nasca times sites were distributed in the lower valley, in the zone of filtration, and in the upper valley. In the lower Nasca Valley is found Cahuachi, the major ceremonial center (Silverman 1993), along with numerous cemeteries (Ogburn 1993). It is no surprise to us that this region was sacred to the prehistoric inhabitants of the region: the emergence of the river at Las Cañas, in the midst of some of the driest territory on the coast of Peru, must have had great symbolic or religious significance. Permanent habitation sites seem to be lacking in the lower valley in Early Nasca times, probably owing to the heat and wind.

In contrast, numerous habitation sites, mostly small villages, were located in the zones of infiltration and in the upper portions of the Aja, Tierras Blancas, and Las Trancas valleys, and in the zone of infiltration of the Taruga Valley. The extensive occupation of the zone of infiltration suggests that water was relatively plentiful in Early Nasca times, and that there were no extended periods of drought that would cause people to move to higher elevations in search of water. In con-

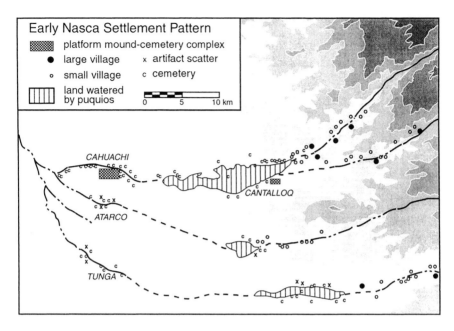

Figure 9.2 Settlement patterns of the Early Nasca Period.

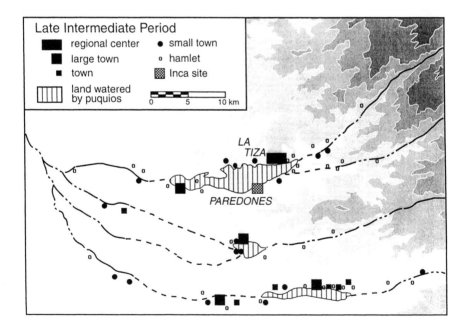

Figure 9.3 Settlement patterns of the Late Intermediate Period.

trast, not a single habitation site is found in any of the dry middle valleys, although numerous cemeteries and two small ceremonial centers (Pueblo Viejo and Cantalloq) were present in the Nasca Valley.

In sum, settlement patterns of the Early Nasca Period match our expectations of settlement locations in a period prior to the construction of the puquios. The lack of permanent occupation of the middle valleys indicates to us that the puquios probably were not yet in use at this time.

This pattern changed completely by the Late Intermediate Period; settlements are found distributed throughout the dry middle zone of all three valleys. The sites in the zones of infiltration and upper valleys are smaller and fewer in number than those in the middle valleys, indicating that the majority of the population lived in the middle valleys. These data indicate quite clearly that puquios were in use by the Late Intermediate Period, and long before the arrival of the Spanish. Furthermore, immediately after, in the Late Horizon, the Incas established a major center at Paredones, in the heart of the dry zone (see figure 9.3). Water must have been available at or near the site; at present, the land in front of Paredones is watered by the puquio, La Gobernadora, and water for domestic purposes was available at the nearby puquio, Pangaraví. It is probably no accident that the Spanish also chose this portion of the valley for their town.

These differences in settlement distribution demonstrate to us that puquios were not in prior to about AD 400, but they were being used to tap subsurface water in the Late Intermediate Period, well before the Inca arrival in AD 1476. Can we, however, be any more precise as to the period of construction within that elapsed millennium? We should be able to estimate the period of initial use by determining during which period people first established permanent settlements in the dry middle valley.

The settlement data from all three valleys suggest that initial use of puquios may have begun by EIP 5 (Transitional Nasca; figure 9.4). In the Nasca Valley, two villages and one town were first established in the middle valley in EIP 5. The middle Taruga Valley includes a very large EIP 5 site, and several EIP 5 villages were established in the middle Las Trancas Valley as well. The association of an EIP 5 site with the puquio Totoral, and EIP 5-6 ceramics found on the berm of the puquio Pangaraví, also support the interpretation that at least some puquios were in use at this time.

It is also apparent that while people were moving down into the middle valley, people were also moving farther up-valley in EIP 5. New and larger settlements were established at elevations above 1,050 meters above sea level in the Aja Valley, and above 1,150 meters above sea level in the Tierras Blancas Valley.

The shift in settlement locations is even clearer by EIP 6-7 times (Late Nasca; figure 9.5). There was a marked change from the pattern of numerous, scattered small villages seen in Early Nasca times to a pattern characterized by a small number of very large towns. In the middle Nasca Valley there is a large site with a nearby village; in the upper Tierras Blancas is another very large site, with two

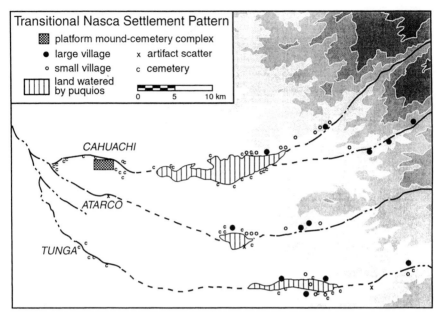

Figure 9.4 Settlement patterns of the Transitional Nasca Period.

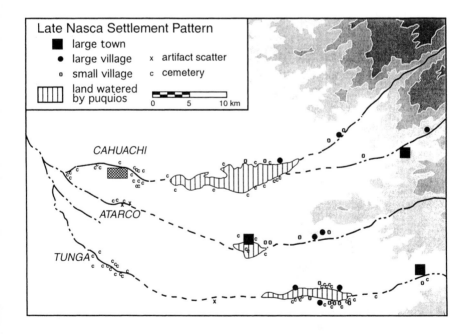

Figure 9.5 Settlement patterns of the Late Nasca Period.

smaller communities nearby. In the middle Taruga Valley the large Nasca 5 site grew to cover some 16 hectares, making it the largest site in the region in Late Nasca times (Schreiber and Isla 1995). In the middle Las Trancas Valley a town and several large villages were occupied in the Late Nasca Period, and a very large site was established in the upper valley. Our data indicate that the Late Nasca Period was a time of population aggregation and perhaps increased sociopolitical complexity. More to the point, the location of major sites in the dry middle valleys indicates quite clearly a reliance on subsurface water, and hence the use of puquios in Late Nasca times.

Movement out of the zone of infiltration and into the upper valley is a pattern that might be expected during periods of prolonged drought. Such a prolonged drought might account for the need to develop new sources of water, such as puquios.

Prehistoric precipitation in the south highlands of Peru has been documented through the study of ice cores by Thompson et al. (1985; Thompson and Mosley-Thompson 1989)). Those data do not yet extend to periods prior to AD 470, but they do indicate a prolonged drought between AD 540 and 560, an especially severe drought between 570 and 610, and another drought between 650 and 730. Menzel (1971) noted evidence of an unusually dry climate in stratified deposits dating to EIP 7. Thus puquio construction in the latter phases of the Early Intermediate Period may be related to an absence of rainfall in the sierra, which would in turn reduce or even eliminate the meager quantities of water that flowed down the southern Nasca tributaries.

Iconographic evidence

The iconography depicted on Nasca ceramics during the Early Intermediate Period underwent significant changes, especially beginning in EIP 5. The Nasca 5 style represents a transitional phase between the older "monumental" styles, Nasca 2-4, and the later "proliferous" styles, Nasca 6-7 (Proulx 2000; Roark 1965). Suzette Doyon (personal communication 2002) finds that many of the elements added to motifs in the latter three phases of the EIP represent the channeling or pooling of water. The appearance of new water-related motifs in EIP 5-7 is an interesting correlation with the apparent construction of puquios, new sources of water, at the same time.

One specific image draws our attention: the orca, or killer whale. In Early Nasca styles it assumes the natural form of the animal, but is it anthropomorphized through the addition of human hands. In its hand it holds either a knife or a human trophy head, and on its teeth are seen drops of blood. While most elements in Nasca art are carefully and precisely drawn, and outlined in fine black lines, blood is depicted as irregular red lines, squiggles, or dots without black outlines.

In Nasca 5 the orca is sometimes depicted in a more geometric, abstract form, but still complete with body, tail, and fins. By the end of this phase, however, the orca has lost most of its body, and it becomes a head with a large, three-sided open mouth with only vestiges of teeth. Emanating from this mouth is a great quantity of blood, represented by irregular, swirling red lines without black outlining (figure 9.6). In Nasca 6-7 this image becomes even more vivid, as the flowing blood comes to dominate the motif.

We suggest that this open form, from which blood emanates, may represent a puquio, from which water emanates out of the ground. The association of the orca with water is obvious. But the fluid flowing out of the orca may also represent water. The life-sustaining fluid (blood) of the animal is analogous to the life-sustaining fluid (water) that sustains the land and the plants grown on it. Continued study of water-related iconography in the latter phases of the EIP may allow us to clarify this argument further.

Figure 9.6 Nasca 5 depiction of the orca.

Radiocarbon assays

Before moving to the questions of a possible historic date for puquio construction, we should add some comments on the utility of radiocarbon assays in dating the puquios. As we have seen, many of the puquios have wooden beams in their ceilings and lining their *ojos*. An obvious means of dating the puquios might be to date these beams through radiocarbon assay. However, as we have also seen, wood eventually deteriorates, and wooden beams are regularly replaced; dating those beams is not likely to indicate the date of construction of the puquio. Moreover, many of the wooden beams are found in galleries of filled-trench construction. As we discuss in more detail below, the episode of trench filling may be relatively recent, in which case dating those beams cannot provide us with the date of the original construction of the puquio. So at the outset we anticipate that radiocarbon assays of wooden beams found in puquios will yield problematic dates.

We can see from the few dates that have been obtained that our fears are warranted. Wooden lintels from the Cantalloq and Majoro puquios, collected by Hermann Trimborn, yielded dates of 110 +/-100 B.P. and 140 +/- 100 B.P. (see Scharpenseel and Pietig 1974), or, roughly the early to mid-nineteenth century. Another sample of a wooden beam was collected from the puquio Bisambra in 1986, during the CORDEICA-sponsored cleaning. The worker who retrieved the beam said it was the oldest piece of wood in the puquio, and that it was "certainly put there by the Incas when they built the puquio." However, similar to Trimborn's dates, that sample yielded a date of only 124 +/- 65 B.P. (SMU 2237; wood), somewhere in the early nineteenth century.

Finally, Clarkson and Dorn (1995) have attempted to date the puquios through assays of samples of desert varnish, which forms on stones in desert environments (see also Bray 1992). However, questions have been raised as to the accuracy of such dating, so we must await further development of the technique before applying it to this case.

Summary of archaeological evidence

The evidence of associated archaeological remains and changes in settlement locations indicate that possibly as early as EIP 5 the ancient people of Nasca began to rely increasingly on subsurface water. The construction of puquios allowed them to tap the phreatic layer, and use that water to irrigate their fields. We also find evidence of rapid population growth, especially in the Late Intermediate Period. It is not unlikely that the puquios grew in number as time went by, reaching nearly their maximum number in the LIP.

Evidence for a Colonial Period Date of Construction

Recently Barnes and Fleming (1991; Barnes 1992; Fleming and Barnes 1994) have argued that the Nasca puquios are not an indigenous development at all, but rather were a form of technology introduced by the Spanish from the Old World. They base their argument on two lines of reasoning. First, as is well known, filtration gallery technology existed in the Old World and was known to the Spanish, and the Spanish in turn built filtration galleries in a number of areas in the New World. Filtration galleries were built in Peru (one in the Santa Valley, six in Surco near Lima, and two in Moquegua) as well as others in Chile, Mexico, and California. Barnes and Fleming (1991; personal communication 1994) have done an admirable job of summarizing the evidence of the use of filtration gallery technology in various places in the New World. However, they then proceed to draw the conclusion that if the Spanish built some of the filtration galleries in the New World, they must have built all of them—even those in Nasca.

We find this line of reasoning to be unconvincing. It denies the possibility, indeed the certainty, that the people of Nasca knew their environment well enough to develop the puquios, that they were aware of the subsurface water and knew how to get at it. The ancient people of Nasca could hardly have missed noticing the river disappearing beneath the surface in the zone of infiltration and its reemergence near Cahuachi, nor failed to realize that the water could be found below the surface in the area between those two points. We see no reason to assume that, just because the technology existed in the Old World, the Spanish must have introduced it to Nasca. As we saw in chapter 1, ancient Andean civilizations developed many ingenious and complex ways to manipulate their environment, including the use of groundwater resources. They did not need to learn this from the Spanish.

As their second line of reasoning, Barnes and Fleming assert that there are simply no references to the puquios in early colonial documents; they find it especially troublesome that the puquios were not described by Cieza and cite his lack of description as evidence that the puquios did not exist. This failure, however, may easily be explained by the fact that Cieza never traveled to the Peruvian south coast (Estrada 1987). He was never in Nasca and could not have had the opportunity to observe the puquios. So we are not surprised that he did not mention them in his descriptions of the south coast. His descriptions of the south coast valleys were a summary of what he was told by some Dominican priests from Chincha; indeed his discussion of the south coast omits the Pisco Valley entirely!

Barnes and Fleming (1991: 55; Fleming and Barnes 1994) believe that the earliest reference to the Nasca puquios refers to events that took place in 1692, regarding rights to the water of Bisambra, and that no earlier references exist. They believe that if the puquios existed at the time of the founding of Nasca (in 1596), there would be mention of them in earlier documents.

While the lack of mention of the puquios in some early documents might be taken at face value to indicate that the puquios did not exist, it is equally possible that some early travelers were simply unaware of their existence, as are many modern travelers. In fact, it is even stranger that, were the puquios built in the sixteenth or seventeenth century by the Spanish, mention of such a major undertaking is entirely lacking. And why, if they only expended the effort to build six filtration galleries near their capital in Lima, did they expend such enormous efforts to build more than forty puquios in the small, out-of-the-way valleys of Nasca?

Indeed, an early description of the puquios does exist, written in 1605 by Reginaldo de Lizárraga (1909). Although Barnes and Fleming mention this source (1991), they did not realize its significance. Lizárraga traveled widely through much of South America, and he was greatly impressed with the dryness of the south coast of Peru. He observed the general lack of water and enumerated available water resources in each valley. He noted where rivers were adequate or not, and in some cases he gave details of irrigation practices. In specific cases he pointed out who built and/or used particular features, distinguishing between the Spanish, the Incas, and the natives (often noting that the latter were very few in number due to the massive postconquest depopulations.)

When he reached Nasca he noted that water was lacking during the highland dry season, but that in the time of the rains the Nasca River was full of water and was quite dangerous. He wrote that during dry seasons the natives *(indios)* drew water from hand-dug pools located at intervals on higher ground. They used that water to irrigate their crops and to sustain themselves until the river flowed again (Lizárraga 1909: 522 [1605]).

It is clear to us that the hand-dug pools located on higher ground must refer to puquios. The sources of irrigation water he describes were distinct from irrigation canals taking water from the river. He was clear that these features were used by natives, and he does not mention either the Spanish or the Incas using them. He also distinguished Nasca from other valleys of the coast of Peru, noting its seasonal lack of river water, and thus the need to rely on some other source of water.

This passage leaves little doubt that the native people of Nasca were using subsurface water prior to the arrival of the Spanish, and the founding of the town of Nasca in 1596. Coupled with the evidence of associated archaeological remains, and changes in settlement patterns, there can be little doubt that the puquios were an indigenous, prehispanic development.

Spanish and Modern Modifications of the Puquios

While it is abundantly clear that puquios were in use long before the Spanish arrived in Nasca, it is not unlikely that they modified the system and perhaps even added to it. Certainly some Spaniards, familiar with filtration galleries in their own country, would have recognized the similarity in puquio technology, and may have seen an opportunity to adapt their own version of that technology to what they found in Nasca.

In spite of having no direct evidence of Spanish-built puquios as yet, we suggest here the possibility that they may have altered several indigenous puquios, and even built one of their own. In chapter 3 (see figure 3.1) we identified two different construction techniques used to build puquios: by digging open trenches and by tunneling. (Many galleries are of filled-trench type but all of these were initially built as open trenches.) These are two very different techniques, requiring different forms of planning and engineering. Is it possible that the two techniques were used by different people, and/or at different times? If we entertain the possibility that tunneling was not a technique used by the prehispanic inhabitants of Nasca, then we can consider the possibility that tunneled puquios or tunneled portions of puquios may be Spanish constructions.

As we have seen, the majority of the puquios were built of open trench construction, but some of them may have been lengthened with tunneled gallery sections. Such lengthening would serve to increase filtrations, and thereby increase the flow of water. In other cases, a tunneled galley branch may have been added to an existing puquio, again to increase the flow of water.

All of the puquios clearly modified in these ways are found in the Aja and Tierras Blancas Irrigation Sectors, and most are in the vicinity of the town of Nasca. The puquios of Llicuas Norte and Majoro each have two branches, the longer of which is of trench construction. In each case a second branch of tunneled construction was added, and each of these new branches leads to, and underneath, the adjacent Nasca riverbed. The puquio La Gobernadora has only a single branch functioning today, but that may have been an addition to a puquio that was of trench construction. The other (trench construction) branch is now abandoned. The long branch of Bisambra (the only branch still in use at present) may have been a tunneled addition to that puquio.

Puquios that may have been lengthened at some point after their initial construction through the addition of a tunneled segment include: (1) the extension of Anglia alongside and under the Aja riverbed, (2) the extension of the southern branch of the puquio Aja alongside and underneath the Aja riverbed, (3) the extension of the southern branch of Huachuca under the Tierras Blancas riverbed, and (4) the extension of Huayrona.

None of the puquios of the Nasca Irrigation Sector show any evidence of modification—all are simple open trenches. Likewise the puquios of the Taruga Irrigation Sector are entirely of trench construction. The puquios of the Las Trancas Irrigation Sector that are still functioning at present are all of trench construction.

Finally, the puquio Cantalloq may be a puquio that was built in its entirety by the Spanish. It lies at the upper extreme of the Tierras Blancas Irrigation Sector. Stratigraphy in the uppermost ojo of the long southern branch indicates that at least the upper portion of the puquio was built by tunneling; the northern branch is tunneled underneath the Tierras Blancas riverbed. Inspection of aerial photographs from 1944 reveals no evidence of berms along the trajectory of the puquio, and thus no evidence of trench construction prior to the creation of the subterranean gallery. Based on our current understanding of the puquios, it would appear that Cantalloq may be only puquio that was built almost entirely by tunneling. If is true that tunneling technology was a Spanish innovation, then Cantalloq is the most likely candidate for a puquio that was built by the Spanish.

The other notable postconstruction modification of the puquios was the filling-in of open trenches to create filled-trench type galleries. Perhaps the construction of tunneled segments of puquios occasioned the realization that the open puquios trenches were taking up valuable space that could be devoted to agricultural fields. Filled-trench galleries mimic tunneled galleries both by providing more surface land for fields and by having access holes—*ojos*—allowing one to enter and clean the galleries. We suggest the possibility that the filling of trenches post-dated the addition of tunneled puquio segments. We also surmise that whenever this trenchfilling took place, trees were much more plentiful in Nasca than they are at present. The number of wooden beams needed to form the ceilings and *ojos* of galleries totaling more than 6 kilometers in length is staggering.

When did this filling take place in absolute terms? González García (1934) noted in several instances that puquios were in a poor state of preservation, and that galleries were falling in. This was most likely the case in filled-trench galleries, and as we have seen many of these have since been cleaned out and left again as open trenches. Thus the filling must have taken place some time before the 1930s, and long enough prior to that time for the wooden ceilings to have begun to deteriorate and collapse. Perhaps the radiocarbon assays from Majoro and Bisambra (see above), both falling in the first half of the nineteenth century, provide us with an approximate date for that filling.

   To reiterate, our evidence indicates that nearly every puquio was built entirely or primarily as an open trench, and used for centuries before the arrival of the Spanish by the native people of Nasca. If the Spanish introduced tunneling techniques, and applied this technology to the Nasca puquios, it may have resulted in the lengthening of several puquios, the addition of branches to others, and perhaps the construction of the puquio Cantalloq.

CHAPTER 10

CONCLUSION:
THE ROLE OF THE PUQUIOS
IN ANCIENT NASCA SOCIETY

In ancient times, before there were aqueducts in the valley, a great drought occurred and the people had no water for years. The people began crying out to their god, Viracocha or Con. They cried and screamed the word nanay (Quechua for "pain"); they were Quechua-speakers. . . . The people went en-mass to the foot of Cerro Blanco, which was their principal templo or adoratorio; this was the place where they spoke to the gods. At that moment, Viracocha/Con descended from the sky to the summit of the mountain and heard the weeping of his people. He was so moved by their cries that he began weeping, and tears flowed from his eyes. The tears ran down Cerro Blanco, penetrated the earth, and these tears were the origin of the aqueducts. (Local legend recorded by Gary Urton in 1982; cited in Clarkson and Dorn 1995: 66)

How does the development of the puquios of Nasca articulate with the trajectory of Nasca cultural history? Did the puquios have anything to do with the radical transformation of local culture between Early and Late Nasca? Were they a cause or an effect of this transformation, or both? We envision the following sequence of events unfolding in prehispanic Nasca, especially in the valleys of Nasca, Taruga, and Las Trancas.

As we saw in chapter 1, there is evidence for very early occupation in the Nasca Valley in the Middle Archaic, at around 6000 BC, but the first large permanent occupations did not occur until the La Puntilla Period, a period during which Chavín was a major influence throughout some parts of the Andean region. During the ensuing Montana Period population grew and settlements were established in all three valleys, but always in places where water was available, never in the middle valleys. A period of conflict seems to have brought this period to a close, and the first florescence of Nasca culture began.

By roughly AD 1, Cahuachi was a major ceremonial site, central to a wide-spread mortuary cult. People made pilgrimages to Cahuachi for religious ceremonies, and to bury their dead in the surrounding cemeteries. Located in the lower Nasca Valley, subject to intense heat and unceasing wind and sandstorms, what made this place special? As we have argued, the reemergence of the Nasca River out of the ground at Las Cañas, and its perennial flow through the zones of Cahuachi and Estaquería to Tambo de Perro, gave this stretch of valley a sacred character. In the rainless coastal desert, where water was a critical limiting resource, water held an important place in the symbolic and religious world of the people. The association of Cahuachi with water can be no accident.

The people who worshipped at Cahuachi lived scattered throughout the Nasca region, and perhaps the Ica Valley. In the southern three tributaries of the Río Grande de Nasca people were restricted to living in the upper portions of the valley, within the Andean foothills, where water was available, but where arable land was in short supply. The northern tributaries were much more suitable for extensive cultivation, and hence human occupation. Most people lived in small villages, and there is little evidence of political centralization. We have suggested that the politicoreligious elites of Nasca society may actually have lived at Cahuachi, where they lived on sacred ground, surrounded by the trappings of power.

And someone had power: the power to organize large groups of people, the power to coordinate major labor projects, and the power to persuade the people to participate in those projects. The physical manifestation of that power is Cahuachi, the construction of its monumental architecture, and the repeated and continuous renewal and enlargement of the platform mounds and pyramids there. In Nasca society there existed not only the power to undertake such projects but also the technical expertise to design and carry them out.

At the same time that Cahuachi enjoyed its florescence, many of the geoglyphs, and probably most of the animal and plant figures, were created. While not requiring huge amounts of labor, they did require precise surveying skills, again indicating a high level of technical expertise in Nasca society (arguments that this technology was introduced from afar by a more advanced society, notwithstanding.)

But by roughly AD 400 something had happened to the Early Nasca culture. What that was, we can only surmise. One factor contributing to the changes we see in the culture may have been a series of devastating droughts that shook Nasca society to its foundations. When rain ceased to fall in the sierra, the rivers did not flow, or the flow was so reduced that human survival was barely possible. And it was so much worse in the southern three tributaries, where already meager river water became harder and harder to find, as the rivers disappeared beneath the surface at points farther and farther upstream. People moved farther up the valleys, into the mountains, trying to mitigate the effects of a deteriorating climate and dwindling water supplies.

Finally the ancient people of Nasca were forced into the only solution possible: they had to find a way to extract water from below the ground. They knew the water was there; they knew where it flowed underground up in the hills, and it still reappeared out of the ground near Cahuachi. They had the technical skills, both architectural and engineering, to design the puquios. And they had the labor, and the coordination, to undertake the project. Rather than devote labor to building and enlarging the monuments at Cahuachi, they turned their efforts to digging puquios.

In Late Nasca times the climate continued to deteriorate, and severe droughts are well documented at this time. The people continued to build puquios to provide themselves with a reliable source of water. Even when the climate improved, which eventually it did, puquios were somewhat less susceptible to fluctuations in rainfall, and hence more reliable, than the rivers. So the people chose to stay in the middle valleys.

But all was not well. Rather than living in small communities, the people aggregated into very large settlements. The simple fact of moving so many people together in much closer proximity than they had known before required new forms of social organization, and new forms of power, not to mention increased opportunities for conflict within and between settlements. But aggregating into large sites, defense against outside hostilities was improved—a single large settlement is easier to defend than a series of small villages. Even the iconography suggests an increase in warfare: there is a marked increase in warriors being painted on ceramics in Nasca 5 and Late Nasca styles. The depictions of the warriors indicate the existence of several different groups, with distinctive clothing and weapons; depictions even include Moche warriors of the north coast. The last centuries of the Early Intermediate Period were a time of conflict in Nasca, and perhaps elsewhere as well.

Why did this conflict take place? While we cannot know the answer to this question at present, we can suggest two contributing factors, which are not mutually exclusive. In the first place, a period of extended drought could have put a strain on all groups in Nasca and surrounding regions. This in turn might increase such hostile actions as the raiding of neighboring areas for life-sustaining resources, as well as the need to protect homes and fields from such raids.

The second contributing factor may have been the puquios, themselves, and the concomitant changes in control over the use of water. Prior to the construction of the puquios, irrigation using river water was probably a fairly simple process in Nasca, involving short canals and small irrigated zones. Major canal systems, requiring labor investment and coordination, did not exist. Each family or village probably had essentially equal access to river water, in those parts of the valley where it was available.

Construction of puquios, however, placed the control of water in the hands of a small number of people: those who controlled the puquios and organized their construction could also restrict the distribution of water from them. Rather than all members of the society having equal access to this life-giving resource, its control was now in the hands of the few. The stage was set for increased conflicts over water and its control, and changes in political and economic power.

While some might argue that these are precisely the conditions that might lead to the emergence of state-level societies, this is not what happened in Nasca. Quite the reverse, the Nasca culture may have fragmented into a series of separate polities, each with its own power structure, and each in conflict with the others. Cahuachi, however, continued in its role as a religious center to which people still made pilgrimages to bury their dead; but, its role as a center of political power was probably over.

We might wonder what would have happened if these events were allowed to unfold without interference from the outside, but this was not to be. Into this milieu of conflict stepped the Wari Empire. By AD 750 Wari was well on its way to establishing political control over much of the central Andes, and for a time this control extended to Nasca. A probable administrative center was built at Pacheco, a site whose lands were watered by the Soisonguito and Soisongo puquios. New Loro culture villages and towns were established in locations not easily defended, suggesting a period of reduced conflict.

After Wari collapsed, and after a brief resurgence of local conflict (perhaps aimed at Wari), Nasca population continued to grow. Perhaps more puquios were built in the Late Intermediate Period to bring more land under cultivation. By the time of the Inca takeover, most local villages and towns were located in and around the parts of the valleys watered by puquios; Nasca society could not have survived without the puquios.

And it seems the Incas were impressed with Nasca. The only settlement they established in the southern tributaries of the Nasca drainage was not administrative in nature; rather, it probably served as a private estate of one of the Inca emperors, perhaps Thupa Inca Yupanqui. What impressed the Inca so much? The three most outstanding features of Nasca, features that would have made a great impression on an Inca, are without a doubt Cerro Blanco, the geoglyphs on the pampa, and the puquios.

Conclusion

We conclude that the puquios were most likely built by the ancient inhabitants of Nasca, beginning with the Nasca culture of the Early Intermediate Period. They may have saved the people from the effects of a devastating drought, and allowed them to continue to live in the Nasca Valley, but the puquios may also have created a new source of conflict, which in turn caused even greater upheavals in Nasca society. Nevertheless, even in later centuries, through the Wari and Inca conquests and up to and including the present, the puquios made life possible in Nasca. They enabled the ancient inhabitants of Nasca to transform the desert into a verdant paradise, and to create the emerald of the Peruvian coast.

BIBLIOGRAPHY

Adams, Robert McC. 1974. "Historic Patterns of Mesopotamian Irrigation Agriculture." In *Irrigation's Impact on Society*, edited by Theodore E. Downing and McGuire Gibson, 1-6. Anthropological Papers of the University of Arizona 25. Tucson: University of Arizona Press.

Barnes, Monica. 1992. "Dating of Nazca Aqueducts." Scientific Correspondence, *Nature* 359: 111.

Barnes, Monica, and David Fleming. 1991. "Filtration-Gallery Irrigation in the Spanish New World." *Latin American Antiquity* 2: 48-68.

Bird, Junius B. 1948. "Preceramic Cultures in Chicama and Virú." In *A Reappraisal of Peruvian Archaeology*, edited by Wendell C. Bennett, 21-28. Society for American Archaeology Memoir 4. *American Antiquity* 13, no. 4, pt. 2.

Bray, Warwick. 1992. "Under the Skin of Nazca." *Nature* 358: 19.

Browne, David M., and José Pablo Baraybar. 1988. "An Archaeological Reconnaissance in the Province of Palpa, Department of Ica, Peru." In *Recent Studies in Pre-Columbian Archaeology*, edited by N. Saunders and O. Montmollin, 299-325. Oxford: BAR International Series 421.

Burger, Richard L. 1992. *Chavín and the Origins of Andean Civilization*. London: Thames and Hudson.

Burger, Richard L., and Lucy Salazar-Burger. 1980. "Ritual and Religion at Huaricoto." *Archaeology* 36: 26-32.

Carmichael, Patrick H. 1991. *Prehistoric Settlement of the Ica-Grande Littoral, Southern Peru*. Report submitted to the Social Sciences and Humanities Research Council of Canada.

Cieza de León, Pedro de. 1984 [1533]. *Crónica del Peru*, primera parte. Lima: Pontificia Universidad Católica del Perú.

Clarkson, Persis B., and Ronald I. Dorn. 1995. "New Chronometric Dates for the Puquios of Nazca, Peru." *Latin American Antiquity* 6: 56-69.

Conlee, Christina. 2000. "Late Prehistoric Occupation of Pajonal Alto: Implications for Imperial Collapse and Societal Reformation." Ph.D. dissertation, Department of Anthropology, University of California, Santa Barbara.

CORDEICA (Corporación de Desarrollo de Ica). 1987. *Proyecto rehabilitación de acueductos arqueológicos de Nasca*. Corporación de Desarrollo de Ica, Consejo de Nasca, y Instituto Nacional de Cultura Dirección General del Patrimonio Cultural y Monumental. Equipo de Asesoramiento y Supervisión Técnica: Ing. Felix Solar La Cruz, Prof. Inv. Josué Lancho Rojas, y Sr. Aroldo Corzo Catalán.

Cushner, Nicholas P. 1980. *Lords of the Land: Sugar, Wine, and Jesuit Estates of Coastal Peru, 1600-1767.* Albany: State University of New York Press.

Day, Kent C. 1974. "Walk-in-Wells and Water Management at Chanchan, Peru." In *The Rise and Fall of Civilizations,* edited by Jeremy Sabloff and C. C. Lamberg-Karlovsky, 182-190. Menlo Park: Cummings.

DeLeonardis, Lisa. 1997. "Paracas Settlement in Callango, Lower Ica Valley, 1st Millennium BC, Peru." Ph.D. dissertation, Department of Anthropology, Catholic University of America, Washington, D.C.

Denevan, William M. 1980. "Configuraciones agrícolas prehispánicas." *América Indígena* 40: 619-652.

Engel, Frédéric. 1958. "Sites et établissements sans céramique de la côte Péruvienne." *Journal de la Société des Americanistes* 46: 67-155.

_____. 1966. *Paracas: Cien siglos de cultura Peruana.* Lima: Editorial Juan Mejía Baca.

Erickson, Clark L. 1985. "Applications of Prehistoric Andean Technology: Experiments in Raised Field Agriculture, Huatta, Lake Titicaca; 1981-2." In *Prehistoric Intensive Agriculture in the Tropics,* edited by Ian Farrington, 209-232. Oxford: British Archaeological Reports, International Series 232.

_____. 1986. "Agricultura en camellones en la cuenca del Lago Titicaca: Aspectos técnicos y su futuro." In *Andenes y camellones en el Perú andina: Historia presente y futuro,* edited by Manual Burga y Carlos de la Torre, 331-350. Lima: CONCYTEC.

_____. 1987. "The Dating of Raised-Field Agriculture in the Lake Titicaca Basin, Peru." In *Pre-Hispanic Agricultural Fields in the Andean Region,* edited by William Denevan, Kent Mathewson, and Gregory Knapp, 373-384. Oxford: British Archaeological Reports, International Series 359.

_____. 1988. "Raised Field Agriculture in the Lake Titicaca Basin: Putting Ancient Agriculture Back to Work." *Expedition* 30, no. 3: 8-16.

Estrada Ycaza, Julio. 1987. *Andanzas de Cieza por tierras americanas.* Guayaquil, Ecuador: Banco Central del Ecuador.

Feldman, Robert A. 1987. "Architectural Evidence for the Development of Nonegalitarian Social Systems in Coastal Peru." In *The Origins and Development of Andean State,* edited by Jonathan Haas, Shelia Pozorski, and Thomas Pozorski, 9-14. Cambridge: Cambridge University Press.

Fleming, David, and Monica Barnes. 1994. "Are the Puquios of Nazca Prehistoric?" Paper presented, General Session, Northern and Western South American Archaeology. Society for American Archaeology, Anaheim, California.

Flores Ochoa, Jorge Aníbal, and Magno Percy Paz Flores. 1985. "La agricultura en lagunas del altiplano." *Ñawpa Pacha* 21: 127-152.

Gasca, Pedro de la. 1976 [1553]. *Descripción del Perú.* Caracas: Universidad Católica Andrés Bello.

Gayton, Anna H., and Alfred L. Kroeber. 1927. The Uhle Pottery Collections from Nazca. *University of California Publications in American Archaeology and Ethnology* 24, no. 1: 1-46.

González García, M. Francisco. 1934. "Los acueductos incaicos de Nazca." *Aguas e Irrigación* 2, no. 2: 207-222.

———. 1978. "Los acueductos incaicos de Nazca." In *Tecnología Andina*, edited by Rogger Ravines, 128-156. Lima: Instituto de Estudios Peruanos.

Hadingham, Evan. 1988. *Lines to the Mountain Gods: Nazca and the Mysteries of Peru*. Norman: University of Oklahoma Press.

Isbell, William H., and Gordon F. McEwan, eds. 1991. *Huari Administrative Structure: Prehistoric Monumental Architecture and State Government*. Washington, D.C.: Dumbarton Oaks.

Isla C., Johny. 1990. "La Esmeralda: Una ocupación del período arcaico en Cahuachi, Nasca." *Gaceta Arqueológica Andina* 5, no. 2: 67-80.

Johnson, David W., Donald A. Proulx, and Stephen B. Mabee. 2002. "The Correlation between Geoglyphs and Subterranean Water Resources in the Río Grande de Nazca Drainage." In *Andean Archaeology II*, edited by Helaine Silverman and William H. Isbell, 307-332. New York: Kluwer Academic/Plenum Publishers.

Kobori, Iwao. 1960. "Human Geography of Methods of Irrigation in the Central Andes." *Andesu, Andes, the Report of the University of Tokyo Scientific Expedition to the Andes in 1958*, 74-97, 417-420. Tokyo: Bijitsu Shuppan sha.

Kolata, Alan L. 1986. "The Foundations of the Tiwanaku State: A View from the Heartland." *American Antiquity* 51: 748-762.

———. 1993. *The Tiwanaku: Portrait of an Andean Civilization*. Cambridge, Mass.: Blackwell.

Kolata, Alan L., and Charles R. Ortloff. 1989. "Thermal Analysis of Tiwanaku Raised Field Systems in the Lake Titicaca Basin of Bolivia." *Journal of Archaeological Science* 16: 233-263.

Kosok, Paul. 1965. *Life, Land and Water in Ancient Peru*. New York: Long Island University Press.

Kroeber, Alfred L. 1956. "Toward Definition of the Nazca Style." *University of California Publications in American Archaeology and Ethnology* 43, no. 4: 327-432.

Kroeber, Alfred L., and Donald Collier. 1998. *The Archaeology and Pottery of Nazca, Peru: Alfred L. Kroeber's 1926 Expedition*. Edited by Patrick H. Carmichael, with an afterword by Katharina J. Schreiber. Walnut Creek, Calif.: AltaMira Press.

Kus, James. 1984. "The Chicama-Moche Canal: Failure or Success? An Alternative Explanation for an Incomplete Canal." *American Antiquity* 49: 408-415.

Lancho Rojas, Josué. 1986. "Descripción y problemas de mantenimiento y rehabilitación de los acueductos de Nasca." Report submitted to CONCYTEC (Consejo Nacional de Ciencia y Tecnología).

Lizárraga, Reginaldo de. 1909 [1605]. "Descripción breve de toda la tierra del Perú, Tucumán, Río de la Plata y Chile." *Nueva Biblioteca de Autores*

Españoles 15: 485-660. Madrid: Bailly-Bailliére é Hijos Editores.

Markham, Clements R. 1991. *Markham in Peru: The Travels of Clements R. Markham, 1852-1853.* Edited and with an introduction by Peter Blanchard. Austin: University of Texas Press.

Massey, Sarah A. 1991. "Social and Political Leadership in the Lower Ica Valley." In *Paracas Art and Architecture*, edited by Anne Paul, 315-348. Iowa City: University of Iowa Press.

Mejía Xesspe, M. Toribio. 1939. "Acueductos y caminos antiguos de la hoya del Río Grande de Nasca." *Actas y Trabajos Científicos del XXVII Congreso Internacional de Americanistas* 1: 559-569.

Menzel, Dorothy. 1959. "The Inca Occupation of the South Coast of Peru." *Southwestern Journal of Anthropology* 15, no. 2: 125-142.

_____. 1964. "Style and Time in the Middle Horizon." *Ñawpa Pacha* 2: 1-114.

_____. 1971. "Estudios arqueológicos en los valles de Ica, Pisco, Chincha y Cañete." *Arqueología y Sociedad* 6: 1-158.

Menzel, Dorothy, John H. Rowe, and Lawrence E. Dawson. 1964. *The Paracas Pottery of Ica: A Study in Style and Time.* University of California Publications in American Archaeology and Ethnology. Vol. 50. Berkeley: University of California Press.

Montoya, Manuel, Wilfredo García, and Julio Caldas. 1994. *Geología de los cuandrángulos Lomitas, Palpa, Nasca y Puquio.* Boletín 53. Lima: Instituto Geológico Minero y Metalúrgico.

Moseley, Michael E. 1969. "Assessing the Archaeological Significance of Mahamaes." *American Antiquity* 34: 48-50.

_____. 1975. *The Maritime Foundations for Andean Civilization.* Menlo Park: Cummings.

Moseley, Michael E., and Gordon R. Willey. 1973. "Aspero, Peru: A Reexamination of the Site and Its Implications." *American Antiquity* 38: 452-468.

Ogburn, Dennis E. 1993. "The Cemeteries of Nasca." Master's thesis, Department of Anthropology, University of California, Santa Barbara.

ONERN (Oficina Nacional de Evaluación de Recursos Naturales). 1971. *Inventario, evaluación y uso racional de los recursos naturales de la costa: Cuenca del río Grande (Nazca).*

_____. 1973. *Inventario, evaluación y uso racional de los recursos naturales de la costa: Cuenca del río Chicama.*

Orefici, Giuseppe. 1993. *Nasca: Arte e società del popolo dei geoglifi.* Milan: Jaca Book.

Ortloff, Charles R. 1981. "La ingeniería chimú." In *La tecnología en el mundo andino, Tomo I, Subsistencia y mensuración*, edited by Heather Lecthmann and Ana María Soldi, 91-134. Mexico City: Universidad Nacional Autónoma de México, Ciudad Universitaria, México.

_____. 1988. "Canal Builders of Ancient Peru." *Scientific American* 256, no. 12: 67-74.

_____. 1993. "Chimú Hydraulic Technology and Statecraft on the North Coast of Peru, AD 1000-1470." In *Research in Economic Anthropology*, Supplement 7, edited by Vernon Scarborough and Bernard Isaac, 327-367. Greenwich: JAI Press.

_____. 1995. "Surveying and Hydraulic Engineering of the Pre-Columbian Chimú State AD 900-1450." *Cambridge Archaeological Journal* 5: 55-74.

Ortloff, Charles R., and Alan L. Kolata. 1989. "Hydraulic Analysis of Tiwanaku Aqueduct Structures at Lukurmata and Pajchiri, Bolivia." *Journal of Archaeological Science* 16: 513-535.

_____. 1993. "Climate and Collapse: Agro-Ecological Perspectives on the Decline of the Tiwanaku State." *Journal of Archaeological Science* 20: 195-221.

Ortloff, Charles R., Michael E. Moseley, and Robert Feldman. 1982. "Hydraulic Engineering Aspects of the Chicama-Moche Intervalley Canal." *American Antiquity* 48: 572-595.

Parsons, Jeffrey R., and Norbert Psuty. 1974. "Agricultura de chacras hundidas en el antiguo Peru." *Revista del Museo Nacional* 40: 31-54.

_____. 1975. "Sunken Fields and Prehistoric Subsistence on the Peruvian Coast." *American Antiquity* 40: 259-282.

Paul, Anne, ed. 1991. *Paracas Art and Architecture: Object and Context in South Coastal Peru*. Iowa City: University of Iowa Press.

Petersen G., Georg. 1980. *Evolución y desaparición de las altas culturas Paracas-Cahuachi (Nasca)*. Lima: Universidad Nacional Federico Villareal.

Pozorski, Shelia, and Thomas Pozorski. 1979. "Alto Salaverry: A Peruvian Coastal Preceramic Site." *Annals of Carnegie Museum of Natural History* 48: 337-375.

_____. 1987. *Early Settlement and Subsistence in the Casma Valley, Peru*. Iowa City: University of Iowa Press.

Pozorski, Thomas, and Shelia Pozorski. 1982. "Reassessing the Chicama-Moche Intervalley Canal: Comments on 'Hydraulic Engineering Aspects of the Chimu Chicama-Moche Intervalle Canal.'" *American Antiquity* 47: 851-868.

Proulx, Donald A. 2000. "Nasca Ceramic Iconography: An Overview." *Studio Potter* 29, no. 1: 36-43.

Quilter, Jeffrey. 1985. "Architecture and Chronology at El Paraíso, Peru." *Journal of Field Archaeology* 12: 279-297.

Regal, Alberto. 1936. *Los caminos del Inca en el antiguo Peru*. Lima: Sanmarti y Cia.

_____. 1943. "Los acueductos precolombinos de Nasca." *Revista de la Universidad Católica del Perú* 11, nos. 4-5: 210-213.

Reindel, Markus, and Johny Isla Cuadrado. 1999. "Proyecto arqueólogico Palpa; Temporada 1998." Final report submitted to the INC, Lima.

Reindel, Markus, Johny Isla Cuadrado, and Klaus Koschmieder. 1999. "Vorspanische Siedlungen und Bodenzeichnungen in Palpa, Süd-Peru."

Beiträge zur Allgemeinen und Vergleichenden Archäologie. Vol. 19, 313-381. Mainz: Verlag Phillip von Zabern.

Reinhard, Johann. 1986. *The Nazca Lines: A New Perspective on Their Origin and Meaning*. Lima: Editorial Los Pinos E.I.R.L.

Riddell, Francis P., and Lidio Valdez C. 1988. "Hacha y la ocupación temprana de Acarí." *Gaceta Arqueológica Andina* 16: 6-10.

Roark, Richard Paul. 1965. "From Monumental to Proliferous in Nasca Pottery." *Nawpa Pacha* 3:1-92.

Rossel Castro, P. Alberto. 1942. "Sistema de irrigación antigua de Río Grande de Nasca." *Revista del Museo Nacional* 11, no. 2: 196-202.

_____. 1977. *Arqueología sur del Perú*. Lima: Editorial Universo S.A.

Rowe, John H. 1960. "Nuevos datos relativos a la cronología del estilo Nasca." In *Antiguo Perú: espacio y tiempo*, 29-45. Lima: Editorial Juan Mejía Baca.

_____. 1969. "The Sunken Gardens of the Peruvian Coast." *American Antiquity* 34: 320-325.

Satterlee, Dennis R., Michael E. Moseley, David K. Keefer, and Jorge E. Tapia. 2001. "The Miraflores El Niño Disaster: Convergent Catastrophes and Prehistoric Agrarian Change in Southern Peru." *Andean Past* 6: 95-116.

Scharpenseel, H.W., and F. Pietig. 1974. "University of Bonn Natural Radiocarbon Measurements VII." *Radiocarbon* 16, no. 2: 143-165.

Schreiber, Katharina J. 1982. "Exploración arqueológica del Valle Carhuarazo, Lucanas, Ayacucho." Final report submitted to the Instituto Nacional de Cultura, Lima.

_____. 1987. "Proyecto Arqueológico los Pukios de Nasca." Final report submitted to the INC, Lima.

_____. 1990. "Proyecto Nasca Sur 1989." Final report submitted to the INC, Lima.

_____. 1991. "Proyecto Nasca Sur 1990." Final report submitted to the INC, Lima.

_____. 1992. *Wari Imperialism in Middle Horizon*. Anthropological Papers 87, Museum of Anthropology, University of Michigan, Ann Arbor.

_____. 1993. "The Inka Occupation of the Province of Andamarcas Lucanas, Peru." In *Provincial Inka: Archeological Identification of the Impact of the Inka State*, edited by Michael A. Malpass, 77-116. Iowa City: University of Iowa Press.

_____. 1998. "Afterword: Nasca Research since 1926." In *The Archaeology and Pottery of Nazca, Peru: Alfred L. Kroeber's 1926 Expedition*, by Alfred L. Kroeber and Donald Collier, edited by Patrick H. Carmichael, 261-273. Walnut Creek, Calif.: AltaMira Press.

_____. 1999. "Regional Approaches to the Study of Prehistoric Empires: Examples from Ayacucho and Nasca." In *Settlement Patterns Studies in the Americas: Fifty Years since Virú*, edited by Brian R. Billman and Gary M. Feinman, 160-171. Washington, D.C.: Smithsonian Institution Press.

_____. 2000. "Los Wari en su contexto local: Nasca y Sondondo." Boletín de Arqueología PUCP 4 (Huari y Tiwanaku: Modelos vs. Evidencias, Primera Parte): 425-447. Lima, Peru.

Schreiber, Katharina J., and Johny Isla Cuadrado. 1995. "Proyecto Nasca Sur 1994: Excavaciones en Taruga." Final report submitted to the INC, Lima.

_____. 1998. "Proyecto Nasca Sur 1996." Final report submitted to the INC, Lima.

Schreiber, Katharina J., and Josué Lancho Rojas. 1988. "Los puquios de Nasca: Un sistema de galerías filtrantes." Boletín de Lima 59: 51-62.

_____. 1995. "The Puquios of Nasca." Latin American Antiquity 6: 229-254.

Silverman, Helaine. 1985. "Cahuachi: Simplemente monumental." Boletín de Lima 41: 85-95.

_____. 1986. "Cahuachi: An Andean Ceremonial Center." Ph.D. dissertation, Department of Anthropology, University of Texas, Austin.

_____. 1987. "A Nasca 8 Occupation at an Early Nasca Site: The Room of the Posts at Cahuachi." Andean Past 1: 5-55.

_____. 1988. "Cahuachi: Non-urban Cultural Complexity on the South Coast of Peru." Journal of Field Archaeology 15, no. 4: 403-430.

_____. 1990. "The Early Nasca Pilgrimage Center of Cahuachi: Archaeological and Anthropological Perspectives." In The Lines of Nazca, edited by Anthony F. Aveni, 209-244. Philadelphia: American Philosophical Society.

_____. 1992. "Estudio de los patrones de asentamiento y reconstrucción de la antigua sociedad Nasca." Boletín de Lima 82: 33-44.

_____. 1993. Cahuachi in the Ancient Nasca World. Iowa City: University of Iowa Press.

_____. 1994. "Paracas in Nazca: New Data on the Early Horizon Occupation of the Rio Grande de Nazca Drainage, Peru." Latin American Antiquity 5: 359-382.

Smith, Clifford, William Denevan, and Patrick Hamilton. 1968. "Ancient Ridged Fields in the Region of Lake Titicaca." Geographical Journal 134: 353-367.

Solar la Cruz, Félix. 1997. Nasca Filtering Galleries/galerías filtrantes. Lima: Universidad Abraham Valdelomar.

Soldi, Ana María. 1982. La agricultura tradicional en hoyas. Lima: Pontificia Universidad Católica del Perú.

Strong, William Duncan. 1957. Paracas, Nazca, and Tiahuanacoid Cultural Relationships in South Coastal Peru. Memoirs of the Society for American Archaeology, 13.

Tello, Julio C. 1959. Paracas: primera parte. Lima: Empresa Gráfica T. Scheuch.

Tello, Julio C., and Toribio Mejía Xesspe. 1979. Paracas, segunda parte: Cavernas y Necrópolis. Lima: Universidad Nacional de San Marcos.

Thompson, Lonnie G., and E. Mosley-Thompson. 1989. "One-Half Millennia of Tropical Climate Variability as Recorded in the Stratigraphy of the Quelccaya Ice Cap, Peru." In Climate Change in the Eastern Pacific and Western Ameri-

cas, edited by D. Peterson, 15-31. American Geophysical Union Monograph 55. Washington, D.C.: American Geophysical Union.

Thompson, Lonnie G., E. Mosley-Thompson, J. F. Bolzan, and B. R. Koci. 1985. "A 1500-Year Record of Tropical Precipitation in Ice Cores from the Quelccaya Ice Cap, Peru." *Science* 229: 971-973.

Valdez Cárdenas, Lidio M. 1989. *Gentilar: Hábitat y economía prehispánica Nasca*. Universidad Nacional de San Cristóbal de Huamanga y el Consejo Nacional de Ciencia y Tecnología, Lima.

Van Gijseghem, Hendrik. n.d. "Migration, Agency, and Social Change on a Prehistoric Frontier: The Paracas-Nasca Transition in the Southern Nasca Drainage, Peru." Ph.D. dissertation, Department of Anthropology, University of California, Santa Barbara. In progress.

Vaughn, Kevin. 2000. "Archaeological Investigations at Marcaya: A Village Approach to Nasca Sociopolitical and Economic Organization." Ph.D. dissertation, Department of Anthropology, University of California, Santa Barbara.

Williams, Carlos. 1980. "Complejos de pirámides con planta en U, patrón arquitectónico de la costa central." *Revista del Museo Nacional* 44: 95-110.

Wittfogel, Karl. 1957. *Oriental Despotism: A Comparative Study of Total Power*. New Haven, Conn.: Yale University Press.

INDEX

ABOUT THE AUTHORS

Katharina Schreiber is professor of Anthropology at the University of California at Santa Barbara, where she has been a member of the faculty since 1984. She received her Ph.D. in 1978 from Binghamton University, and has taught at the University of Connecticut and the University of Arizona. She began doing archaeological fieldwork in Ayacucho, Peru, in 1974, and she has devoted much of her research to the study of the pre-Inca Wari Empire. She is the author of numerous articles on the Wari Empire, and the book, *Wari Imperialism in Middle Horizon Peru*, published in 1992 by the Museum of Anthropology at the University of Michigan. In the 1980s her focus of field research moved to the Nasca region on Peru's south coast, where she began her investigations of the puquios, in collaboration with Professor Lancho. She undertook several seasons of archaeological survey in the region between 1986 and 1996, and she has documented more than 1,000 previously unrecorded archaeological sites. She is currently working on a monograph, based on those surveys, that traces the development of prehispanic cultures in Nasca from the earliest human occupation to the Spanish conquest.

Josué Lancho Rojas received his training in history, and he was a teacher and public school principal in Nasca from 1967 to 1994. From 1995 to 1999 he was professor of educative investigation and tourism. He served as a member of the Municipal Council of Nasca from 1975 to 1979, and he was the Nasca provincial director of the Peruvian National Institute of Culture from 1982 to 1987. He is the author of two editions of *Nasca: Datos Geográficos e Históricos* (1973, 1987), *Ensayo Histórico de Nasca* (1974; currently being revised for its second edition), and *María Reiche: La Dama de las Pampas* (1974; 2nd edition 2000), among other works. He has served as coordinator or advisor for some sixteen documentary films on the geoglyphs of Nasca between 1977 and the present. His long interest in the Nasca puquios led to his writing a lengthy report, "Descripción y Problema de Mantenimiento y Rehabilitación de los Acueductos," for the Peruvian Council on Science and Technology and the Organization of American States in 1986, and his collaboration with Professor Schreiber in their continued study of the puquios. In 2000 he was responsible for the educational and tourism portions of the UNESCO Master Plan for the Nasca geoglyphs. In recognition of his illustrious record as a teacher and historian, he has been the recipient of many local honors, including a Diploma of Honor from the National Institute of Culture in 1992, the Civic Medal of Nasca in 1994, and again in 1995, and the Golden Shield of the city of Ica in 1998. He is currently working on three books on the archaeology and history of Nasca as well as a book of poetry.